AF540297

MODERN CITY SPACES

MODERN CITY SPACES

Edited by
Anwesha Chattopadhyay

Modern City Spaces

Edition : 2025

ISBN 978-93-91771-35-5

Published by:

CRESCENT PUBLISHING CORPORATION

4806/24, Mathur Lane,
Ansari Road, Darya Ganj,
New Delhi - 110 002
Ph.: 011 - 23244131
Mob.: + 91 - 9711991838, 9999021668
E-mail: crescentbook@gmail.com
Website: www.crescentpublishingcorp.weebly.com

Typesetting by
Priyanka Graphics
New Delhi

Printed at:
Balaji Offset
Delhi

Printed in India

Preface

Scrolling back to Darwinism, we find, Evolution is the change in the characteristics of species over several generations, and it marks its existence in every sphere of life. Turning back the yellow pages of History, it can be observed, that civilisation is a complex culture with five characteristics advanced cities, specialised workers, record keeping, advanced technology and complex institutions.

Scrolling back to Darwinism, we find, Evolution is the change in the characteristics of species over several generations, and it marks its existence in every sphere of life. Turning back the yellow pages of History, it can be observed, that civilisation is a complex culture with five characteristics advanced cities, specialised workers, record keeping, advanced technology and complex institutions.

This book covers multidisciplinary topics that revolve around different aspects of city life. It provides a perfect platform to explore and discuss multifaceted effects of city life on human beings and civilization. Hence it gives us opportunity to acquire knowledge from the thoughts, opinions and understandings of the respected researchers and academicians who pro-actively contributed chapter in this book.

Anwesha Chattopadhyay

*Acknowledgement*

I am thankful to all the contributors who devoted their valuable time, thoughts and energy in creating some enriched piece of writings.

Also, a heartfelt gratitude to the publishing house for giving the privilege to work with them.

It will be unjust if I do not mention the name of my dear friend, Tanaya Majumder, without whose help and support the publication of the book was not possible at the first place.

Contents

List of Contributors

Anwesha Chattopadhyay, Assistant Professor, School of Commerce, Jain (Deemed to be) University, Bangalore. Email id: c.anwesha@jainuniversity.ac.in

Dr. Piyali Basu, Associate Professor, Department of Political Science, Women's Christian College, Kolkata. Email id: piyalibasu1972@gmail.com

Rwiti Biswas, Student, Post Graduate Diploma in Women's and Gender Studies, Indira Gandhi National Open University (IGNOU) and M.A. in English, West Bengal State University (WBSU). Email id: rwitibiswas22@gmail.com

Swastideepa Mazumder, Student, B.Ed, Shri Shikshayatan College, University of Calcutta and M.A. in English, University of Calcutta, Kolkata. Email id: alokananda1802@gmail.com

Dr. Pallavi Sinha Das, Associate Professor, Department of Political Science, Adamas University, Kolkata. Email id: pallavisinhadas@gmail.com

Trisha Bakshi, PhD Research Scholar, Department of Sociology, Vidyasagar University, Midnapore. Email id: trishabksh@gmail.com

Maitreyee Bardhan Roy, Guest Coordinator, Department of Women Studies, Diamond Harbour Women University, Emeritus Professor of Political Science, Adamas University. Email id: maitreyee25@rediffmail.com

ਪ.

Obituary

This is my sincerest condolences for such an incredible loss. I deeply regret of losing such a personality, Dr Bardhan Roy. He was a scientist in Indian Chapter of International Rice Research Institute and he retired as Joint Director from Department of Agriculture, Government of West Bengal. May all his sweet memories help his family and friends to have courage and face all the difficulties ahead. He will always remain in our thoughts and prayers. We always pray that you have a peaceful journey in afterlife.

Chapter 1

Best Student City in India

Anwesha Chattopadhyay

1. Introduction

The concept of Student City is relatively new. Today's students are the future of the society as well as the world. Student population in any city can give a picture of the same city in forthcoming years, also students make a city lively and colourful. Students consume cultural and recreational products in the place where they reside and, in many cases, are producers themselves (Russo et. al., 2003). But not all cities have the fortune of having such population unless the city itself provides enormous opportunities and basic safety. In other words, the city offering the best amenities to the student community is called a student city. Throughout ages, it had been dreams of every single student to visualize themselves completing their graduation with their favourite subject from the best University and fly their graduation caps with all their batchmates in air. Generally, the students from eastern world have a high fascination to step their feet in a western nation for their higher studies. In a country like India, students from rural areas. small towns and suburbs aspire to complete their higher studied in a big metropolitan city so that they get exposure to new opportunities that are unavailable in their place of residence. But right after school life is over, it becomes a tough job for them to decide which universities to apply. It is a life-changing decision and hence it becomes very challenging job for the young minds to come to a conclusion. Previously, students had very less options to explore but the scenario is completely different. There are various subjects in various streams, there are different combinations of subjects now which were unimaginable few years back. It is a great deal for students but on the other side it makes the young students confused about what they want, what is suitable for them, what career prospects will be open to them after they graduate and so on. Hence, the selection of universities or colleges brings a huge amount of brain storming in their lives.

Selection of institutions is a subjective matter and it is performed by each and individual students on the basis of their personal perception. They generally consider the course that will help them to become their dream professional or the institute that provides the best opportunities. They begin their search keeping these aspects in minds, and hence selects the institute first and then move to the city where the institute is situated. What they fail to realise is that, there are other aspects to when it comes to shifting to a place from their home town. They ignore the fact whether the city they are planning to shift is safe or not, whether staying there is affordable or not, whether they will be accepted by the crowd already present there or whether they will be able to pacify themselves to the new speed of life. According to Chatterson P. (2010), the idea of university life as `a great teenage transhumance' still dominates the typical image of student life, and obscures the many students from lower income families who do not fit into this mould. These aspects may sound unimportant to some people, but actually they are not. A place having the best university but lacking safety at night or at any time of the day can never be a preferable option for a young student who is going to stay completely alone in a completely new place for the very first time. Also, a student with a feeble financial background will confront a huge problem in residing in an expensive city. A city producing highest number of successful graduates every year can be extremely unfriendly and unwelcoming to the out-station students. In one word, the 'Best' can never be the best for everyone.

This paper aims to rank few big cities in India favourable for students keeping all these aspects in mind. In other words, this paper is expected to discover the best student city in India, that not only provides quality education and opportunity but also takes into consideration the social factors that help a student to thrive in the city.

2. Review of literature

It is not very difficult to find out the names of the renowned universities in the age of 4G. With one click in Google search, one can find a long list of the top universities in the world. According to Wikipedia, "University rankings of institution in higher education which have been ranked on the basis of various combination of factors". Rankings, most of time are published by various magazines, newspapers, websites etc.

The three most promising and influential global rankings are published by Quacquarelli Symonds (QS), Times Higher Education (THE) and the Shanghai Ranking Consultancy (Academic Ranking of World Universities, ARWU).

- Quacquarelli Symonds (QS) is a British company founded by Nunzio Quacquarelli in 1990. QS world university rankings is an annual publication and it was previously known as Times Higher Education- QS World University Rankings. In 2009, both the ranking bodies got separated, QS continued with the old method while THE introduced a new method of ranking. Name of the editor in Ben Sowter who happens to the Head of Research as well. It is the one and only international ranking who have received the approval of prestigious International Ranking Expert Group (IREG). It is mostly viewed ranking reported by Alexa internet, according to Wikipedia.
- Times Higher Education (THE) is a London-based academic magazine published weekly. It was formerly known as Times Higher Education Supplement (THES) and its first issue took place in the year 1971. Name of the editor of this magazine is John Gill. Although the news is not confirmed yet but there was a rumour in 2019 that the partner of THE, Elsevier had a plan to take of THE completely. In 2004, it first published the University rankings which was known as Times

Higher Education- QS World University Rankings. It is evident that QS was a partner at that time and got separated in 2009, it was then when THE tied up with Thomson Reuters.

- Academic Ranking of World Universities (ARWU) publishes the world ranking of universities every year. In 2003, it made its first rankings which was issued by Shanghai Jiao Tong University. It has gained great popularity for its methodology, transparency and unbiasedness towards Asian institutions, although it belongs to China. From 2009, Shanghai Ranking Consultancy is an independent body that focuses only on academic matters and ARWU has been published and copyrighted by this consultancy since then. In 2011, a board was set up with members like scholars, academicians and policy researchers to have their perspectives to make the rankings even better.

Student city: Finding the best university for oneself is the first and foremost criteria and that can be solved by the ranking lists available one click away from anyone and everyone. But it is only one criterial, there are other parameters for the students to be taken care of. When they decide to fly abroad, it is obvious that they have to stay somewhere in the new city, so they also need to know whether surviving in the new city is possible for them or not. In other words, they need to know if they can easily afford to stay in the new country. Apart from that, some students seek review of ex-students of the universities they are looking for. There comes the concept of Student City.

Quacquarelli Symonds (QS) had introduced the Best Student ranking to bring forward the best option to the international students. According to QS, students have the right to know the perfect urban destination for studying alongside the University. QS have a unique style of ranking the cities in terms of some indicators that they find to be very essential for any pupil.

Indicators for preparing the ranking list: Five key categories were considered till 2016. They are University Ranking, Student Mix, Desirability, Employer Activity and Affordability. From 2017, another category was added, which is called Student review. Each of the indicators are explained vividly in this section. Each indicator is given equal weightage as they are considered to have equal Importance.

1. University Ranking: There already exists a ranking list of Universities published by QS. Those ranked universities play the most important role in constructing the index of this indicator. The number of ranked universities in a particular city is counted and the cumulative performance of all such institutions are taken into account. According to this collective performance another ranking list is prepared and thus the score given to the city on the basis of University ranking depends on the range of this new ranking. It is described briefly in the following table. In the first column, we have the ranges of the new ranks acquired from all the ranked universities of a particular city and the second column refers the score of the city.

Table 2.1: QS scoring system for University rankings

Range	*Score*
1-10	100
11-25	50
26-50	30
51-100	20
101-200	10
201-300	5
301-400	3
401-500	2
501+	1

Source: QS website

2. Student Mix: This indicator was included keeping into mind that how much a city is student-friendly. According to QS, the cities having higher proportion of students in the population is likely to be more welcoming students from all over the world and every student should love the environment than anything else anywhere. The simplest indicator would be the ratio of total number of students in the city to the total population of the city. But the indicators considered here are little more refined.

- International volume: It is defined as the number total number of international students in the QS ranked universities.
- International ratio: It is defined as the proportion of international students out of all the students enrolled in the QS ranked universities.
- Tolerance and inclusion: This category is defined as the environment in which a student will not miss his or her cultural lifestyle and background. In other words, the population mix in the city will be such that the students feel comfortable just like their home town. This indicator is governed by Social Progress index.

3. Desirability: This category deals with the sustainability of cities. By sustainable, we not only mean the environmental issue, there are other issues too. In fact there are diverse factors such as safety, opportunity and corruption. In simpler words, the students and their parents look for a city which is liveable.

First and foremost, criterion is the economic and social factor. These are determined by a number of indices.

- The first among them is Global Liveability Index. It is published by The Economist Intelligence Unit. This index refers to the location with respect to it living conditions, the ranking provides world's best and worst living conditions. There are five broad categories, namely Stability, Education, Healthcare facilities, Culture and Environment and lastly, Infrastructure. Under these broad divisions, there are 30 factors, both qualitative and quantitative.
- The second is Globalisation and World City Index (GaWC), "the leading academic thinktank on cities in globalization". It is based in the geography department of Loughborough University in Leicestershire, United

Kingdom. The ranking is based on their connectivity through four "advanced producer services" which are accountancy, advertising, banking/finance and law. Economic factors are given more importance than political or cultural factors.

- Third is PwC's Cities of Opportunity Index which is an indicator of the social and economic health of 30 of the world's leading business cities. It creates a balance between these two factors. The key measures include economic clout, ease of doing business, education, technology readiness, location, access, transportation and infrastructure, demographics and liveability, and cost. Along with these economic features, equal importance is given to social features like good quality of life, senior wellbeing, housing, and disaster preparedness.
- Then comes the Global Power City Index (GPCI). Its main objective is to judge magnetism of a city, or in other words the capacity to attract people from foreign land. Six main key features are taken into consideration, Economy, Liveability, Cultural mixing, Research and Development, Environment and Accessibility.
- The City Momentum Index presents cities with the strongest positive momentum in their economies and real estate markets over the short to medium term make place for themselves in this list.
- Trip Advisor's History & Culture List or TripAdvisor's Shopping List gives the best destinations throughout the world. This adds 5 points to the total point.

Apart from the economic factors and indices to judge a city, next comes the safety about which both students and their parents are concerned with. For this criterion as well, there are couple of indices like Safety Index compiled by Numbeo (the inverse of the crime index), Corruption Perception index to assess the presence of corruption in public sector and a pollution score to measure the environmental sustainability.

4. Employer activity: This factor speaks about the recruitment opportunities in a city after graduation. Domestic and International Employer Popularity are the two measures considered here. The first determines the number of domestic employers who identified at least one institution in the city as producing excellent graduates and the second one on the weighted count of international employers who identified at least one institution in the city for giving outstanding graduates.

5. Affordability: The category name itself describes its criterion. Tuition fee is the most important factor here. The tuition fees of the universities are taken into account. Apart from that, Mercer's Cost of living index of the cities, Ipad index by Commsec and well known index of retail pricing by the Economist Intelligence Unit are included to understand how the city is affordable for students coming from different financial backgrounds.

6. Student's View: This indicator is based on a student survey which collected over 85,000 responses worldwide. It provides students with an opportunity to share their experience of studying and staying in a particular city. Students rate on eight different categories: tolerance and inclusion, affordability, diversity, friendliness, ease of getting around, nightlife, employment opportunities, arts and culture. Also, the students who stayed after completed graduation in that city were also surveyed.

Compilation: Each indicator is converted into an ordinal number by assigning ranks to the results and subtracting the rank of each result from the maximum rank. The resulting scores are combined with certain weights that are determined relatively from the scores and scaled to the top-performing city in the category to give a score with a maximum of 100 for each category, which are then summed to produce the final score, out of a theoretical maximum of 600. The following table presents the first 10 student cities in the world and four student cities of India that are listed (2019) in the ranking.

Table 2.2: QS rankings of student cities

Rank	*City*	*Overall score*	*University ranking*	*Student mix*	*Desirability*	*Employer activity*	*Affordability*	*Student view*
1	London	485	100	92	84	93	22	94
2	Tokyo	480	83	59	100	100	53	85
3	Melbourne	475	69	100	92	88	27	99
4	Munich	474	54	87	90	80	62	100
5	Berlin	464	50	79	89	80	67	98
6	Montreal	459	57	92	90	78	43	99
7	Paris	458	80	80	86	88	41	82
8	Zurich	456	63	84	96	90	43	80
9	Sydney	455	65	97	99	86	22	86
10	Seoul	454	85	72	99	80	41	85
10	Hongkong SAR	454	81	80	72	99	54	81
81	Bangalore	250	33	8	35	34	84	56
85	Mumbai	244	34	8	43	66	48	45
113	Delhi	190	36	10	29	30	69	17
115	Chennai	185	24	9	31	41	63	18

Source: QS website

3. Research Gap

Few papers are found on the influence of student communities in the student cities of European countries. Apart from that, this area of research is unexplored. As far as Indian cities are concerned, we can find various news articles which can guide students to enrol themselves in appropriate institutions, but no academic research whatsoever has been done on it. This concept is largely ignored in the world of research.

4. Research Objective

QS ranking of student cities played a major role to influence the researcher. The various aspects that have been considered are basically the ground factors that student tend to ignore. Hence, the international list that QS has structured brought the idea that same can be constructed for the students residing in small towns or villages or semi-urban suburbs who dream to have a career in big cities of India. The objective of this paper is to find out the best student city in India.

5. Research Design

Type of data: Both primary and secondary data

Source of secondary data: UniRank, Numbeo.

Sampling unit for primary data collection: Students

Sample size:

Type of sampling: Convenient sampling and snowball sampling

Toll used for data collection: Questionnaire

Analysis: Maintaining a parity with QS rankings, the factors here considered are University ranking, Affordability, Safety and security and Students' choice. Points will be allotted to each city on the basis of these factors and then are added to calculate the total. Depending on the total, the rank list will be prepared.

6. Evaluation of cities to find the best student city in India

A primary survey presented name of six cities of India to be chosen by maximum number of students. In the study, those six cities and selected for ranking, namely, Bangalore, Chennai, New Delhi, Kolkata, Hyderabad and Mumbai.

I. University ranking

This factor is the most important one as quality of education matters a lot for an individual as well as for a nation. For this first factor, UniRank is used. UniRank is a university search engine that was established in the year 2005, it provides reviews and rankings of over 13723 universities and colleges in 200 countries. UniRank has ranked 878 universities and colleges in India that belong to various cities. The criteria followed by UniRank are as follows.

i) The institutions should be accredited, licensed or chartered by any prestigious and recognised Indian University or higher education-related organization.

ii) The institutions should offer at least 4 years UG program or PG program, either Masters or PhD.

iii) The courses should not be distance learning, there should prevail proper classroom training, traditional teacher-student face-to-face interaction.

Based on these criteria, University of Delhi tops the list in the year 2020, followed by Indian Institute of Technology Bombay (IITB) and Kanpur (IITK) in second and third position.

Hence, we will be allotting points to the respective cities based on data provided by UniRank in two ways. First, we search for cities having maximum number of ranked institution and second, the cities having higher ranked universities. The points allotment technique is explained in tables 1 and 2.

Table 6.1.1: Point allotment based on rank of institutions

Number of ranked institutes	*Points allotted*
50 and above	10
40-50	9
35-40	8
30-35	7
25-30	6
20-25	5
15-20	4
10-15	3
5-10	2
Below 5	1

Table 6.1.2: Point allotment based on rank of institutions

Rank of institutes	*Points allotted*
0-10	10
10-50	9
50-100	8
100-200	7
200-300	6
300-400	5
400-500	4
500-600	3
600-700	2
700 and above	1

According to the data available in UniRank website, we assign points to the six cities under study. Table 6.1.3 and 6.1.4 has the respective points while table 6.1.5 has the final points on a total of 20 for this criterion.

Table 6.1.3: Point allotment of the six cities based on Number of ranked

Name of city	*Number of ranked institutions*	*Points allotted*
Bangalore	22	5
Chennai	25	5
Hyderabad	16	4
Kolkata	16	4
Mumbai	14	3
New Delhi	24	5

Table 6.1.4: Point allotment of the six cities based on Higher ranked institutions

Name of city	*Highest ranked institution*	*Rank*	*Points allotted*
Bangalore	Indian Institute of Science	16	9
Chennai	Indian Institute of Technology Madras00	4	10
Hyderabad	International Institute of Information Technology, Hyderabad	18	9
Kolkata	Indian Statistical Institute	31	9
Mumbai	Indian Institute of Technology Bombay	2	10
New Delhi	University of Delhi	1	10

Table 6.1.5: Total points earned by each city based on University rankings

Name of city	*Total points (out of 20)*
Bangalore	14
Chennai	15
Hyderabad	13
Kolkata	13
Mumbai	13
New Delhi	15

II. Affordability

By affordability, we mean the minimum cost of the factors like rent, food etc in a city for those who are coming from a different place. Cost of living Index is the considered to be the representative of this factor along with Rent Index and Groceries Index. All these data, current and accurate are available in the world's largest database of users, Numbeo. It provides detailed information about all cities and countries. According to Numbeo, "Cost of Living Index (Excl. Rent) is a relative indicator of consumer goods prices, including groceries, restaurants, transportation and utilities. Cost of Living Index does not include accommodation expenses such as rent or mortgage. If a city has a Cost of Living Index of 120, it means Numbeo has estimated it is 20% more expensive than New York (excluding rent)". The figures that are used in our research represent Cost of Living Index of mid-year 2020.

Apart from Cost of Living Index, Numbeo provides data on Rent Index, Groceries Index, Restaurant Index and Local Purchasing Power Index. Rent and groceries are the indispensable part of life, especially for those who are arriving from different place to stay in a specific city. Hence, the inclusion of these indices seems to be a necessity.

Rent Index is an estimation of prices of renting any place for living, specifically apartments in a city compared to New York City. For example, if Rent index of a city is 70, that implies Numbeo has estimated that the rents of apartments in that city is on average 30% less than the rent in New York.

Similarly, Groceries Index is an estimation of prices of grocery in any city compared to New York City. Calculations are done exactly in the similar manner. In this section, Numbeo uses the weights of items or commodities in the "Markets" section for each city.

Cost of living index is highest in Gurgaon with a score of 29.92 and minimum at Thiruvananthapuram with a score of 19.85. Groceries index is highest in Chandigarh with a score of 31.91 and minimum at Lucknow with a score of 20.97. On the basis on the maximum and minimum values, points are allotted to all the cities. Similar method is applied for Rent index. It has a peculiar data which is clearly visible from diagram 6.2.1. Here it is observed that the rent index ranges from 3 to 10 whereas it is abnormally high for Mumbai which is 19.56. It could be considered as an outlier, but this city is an important one in our study, hence cannot ignore its presence or importance. The point allotment is done in the usual way to keep the originality of the data.

Figure 6.2.1: Bar plot of the rent index of the Indian cities

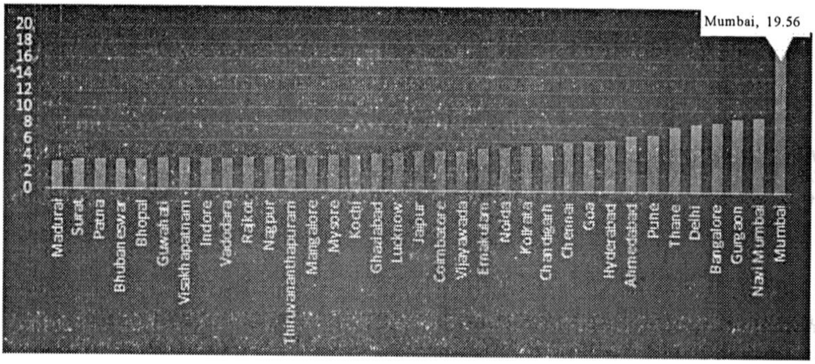

The following tables exhibit the point allotment of the cities considering the maximum and minimum of each cities.

Table 6.2.1: Point allotment based on CLIN

Rent index	*Points allotted*
0-2	10
2-4	9
4-6	8
6-8	7
8-10	6
10-12	5
12-14	4
14-16	3
16-18	2
18-20	1

Table 6.2.2: Point allotment based on Rent index

Groceries index	*Points allotted*
20-20.9	10
21-21.9	9
22-22.9	8
23-23.9	7
24-24.9	6
25-25.9	5
26-26.9	4
27-27.9	3
28-28.9	2
29 and above	1

Table 6.2.3: Point allotment based on Groceries index

CLIN	*Points allotted*
19-19.9	10
20-20.9	9
21-21.9	8
22-22.9	7
23-23.9	6
24-24.9	5
25-25.9	4
26-26.9	3
27-27.9	2
28 and above	1

Based on the point table 6.2.1, the selected cities are given the points. The cities being cosmopolitan in nature, cost of living index are high, Mumbai being the highest. So, affordability in these important cities is less than other small cities and towns in India. Among the six cities considered in our study, Kolkata and Hyderabad exhibits more affordability.

Table 6.2.4: Points of the six cities based on Cost of Living Index

Name of city	*Cost of Living Index*	*Points*
Bangalore	26.98	2
Chennai	27.74	2
Hyderabad	25.69	4
Kolkata	25.26	4
Mumbai	28.87	1
New Delhi	27.43	2

Based on the table 6.2.2, we have the following points for each and individual cities. Mumbai is the most expensive city as far as rent is concerned. Kolkata is most affordable among the cities that had been studied in the research.

Table 6.2.5: Points of the six cities based on Rent Index

Name of city	*Rent Index*	*Points*
Bangalore	8.39	6
Chennai	6.05	7
Hyderabad	6.35	7
Kolkata	5.51	8
Mumbai	19.56	1
New Delhi	8.25	6

Based on the table 6.2.3, we have the following points for each and individual cities. Mumbai is the most expensive city for groceries as well. New Delhi is most affordable among the cities that had been studied in the research, followed by Chennai.

Table 6.2.6: Points of the six cities based on Groceries Index

Name of city	*Groceries Index*	*Points*
Bangalore	27.68	3
Chennai	25.96	4
Hyderabad	27.10	3
Kolkata	26.74	4
Mumbai	28.83	2
New Delhi	25.54	5

The final score of each city considering all these three indices is presented in the table 6.2.7. the score is calculated out of 30.

Table 6.2.7: Total points earned by each city based on Affordability

Name of city	*Total points (out of 30)*
Bangalore	11
Chennai	13
Hyderabad	14
Kolkata	16
Mumbai	4
New Delhi	13

III. Safety and security

Crime Index, listed by Numbeo is supposed to be an estimation of overall level of crime in a given city or a country. Crime levels lower than 20 is considered here as very low, crime levels between 20 and 40 as low, crime levels between 40 and 60 as moderate, crime levels between 60 and 80 as high and finally crime levels higher than 80 as very high. Safety index is defined as the opposite of crime index. If the city has a very high safety index, it is defined as a very safe city. Safety index is highest in Mangalore with a score of 74.33 and lowest in Ghaziabad with a score of 38.1. Depending on this maximum and minimum values, the points are to be allotted in the following manner.

Table 6.3.1: Point allotment based on Safety index

Safety index	*Points allotted*
74-78	10
70-74	9
66-70	8
62-66	7
58-62	6
54-58	5
50-54	4
46-50	3
42-46	2
38-42	1

Based on the above table, points are allotted to the cities under study. Chennai is the safest while New Delhi is the least safe city under our consideration.

Table 6.3.2: Total points earned by each city based on Safety and Security

Name of city	*Safety Index*	*Points (out of 10)*
Bangalore	45.92	2
Chennai	59.67	6
Hyderabad	56.03	5
Kolkata	47.91	3
Mumbai	56.87	5
New Delhi	40.82	1

IV. Students choice

For this criterion, a primary survey has been conducted. Tool used for collection of data is a questionnaire asking about preferable citied for higher studies. Questionnaire has been distributed by email to students of all zones of the country as far as possible including the northern, southern, eastern, western and north-eastern states of India. The result of this study totally depends on the students who have filled up the questionnaire. There are 732 respondents of this study and the result is presented in the figure 6.4.1. Most of the students have preferred to study in Bangalore while the least popular city here is Chennai. Points are allotted according to the ranks.

Figure 6.4.1: Pie chart showing the students' preference of cities

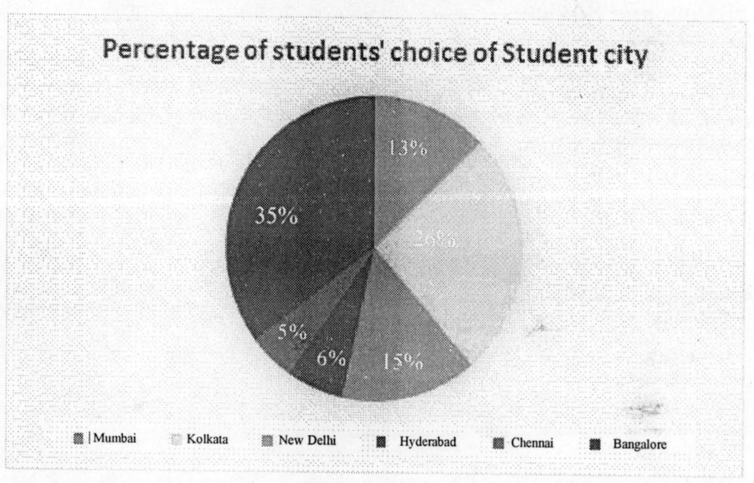

Table 6.4.1: Points scored by cities based on Students' choice

Name of city	*Choice percentage*	*Rank*	*Points (out of 10)*
Bangalore	35%	1	10
Kolkata	26%	2	9
New Delhi	15%	3	8
Mumbai	13%	4	7
Hyderabad	6%	5	6
Chennai	5%	6	5

7. Compilation and Conclusion

Now it is time to compute the total of all the cities and find out the best student city according to our research. Before reaching to any conclusion, let us throw some light on the limitations of the study. The research is mainly based on secondary data, available in internet. Apart from that, there are other criteria like cultural mix of students or employer activity could have been included, but due to lack of proper information, these were excluded.

The scores of the four factors, University ranking, Affordability, Safety and Students' choice are to be added and the ranks to be given to each city.

Table 7.1: Best Student City of India

Name of City	*University Ranking*	*Afforda-bility*	*Safety and Security*	*Students' choice*	*Total (out of 70)*	*Ranks*
Kolkata	13	16	3	9	41	1
Chennai	15	13	6	5	39	2
Hyderabad	13	14	5	6	38	3
New Delhi	15	13	1	8	37	4
Bangalore	14	11	2	10	37	4
Mumbai	13	4	5	7	29	6

According to our study, Kolkata is the best student city in India followed by Chennai and Hyderabad in second and third position respectively. Bangalore, although holds number one position in popularity among students shared fourth rank along with New Delhi who has the highest university ranking. Mumbai's affordability is very low compared to other cities under study and this particular factor has brought it to the sixth position.

8. Scope of further study

As mentioned earlier, more factors can be included in the study. Also, for achieving result with better clarification, appropriate weights can be attached with each factor depending on their importance. Obviously, possibility of inclusion of more Indian cities cannot be ruled out.

References

Chatterson P. (2010), The student city: an ongoing story of neoliberalism, gentrification, and commodification, Environment and Planning A 2010, volume 42, pages 509 - 514.

Russo A, Berg L, Lavanga M (2003), The Student City: Strategic Planning for Student Communities in EU Cities, Paper submitted to the R-sections of the 43rd European Congress of the Regional Science Association, Jyväskylä, Finland August 27-30 2003.

Numbeo

QS Ranking

UniRank

Wikipedia

Chapter 2

Smart Cities: An Indian Perspective

Dr. Piyali Basu

Introduction

Since the industrial revolution, cities have been the engines of economic growth. Urbanization, predominantly measured by shift in population from rural to urban settlements, is an integral part of economic progress and a phenomenon experienced by almost all the countries round the globe. The United Nations estimated that by 2030, over 60% of the global population will be living in cities or peri-urban communities that are increasingly concentrated in Asia, Africa, and Latin America. (United Nations, the 2014 revision: Highlights," 2015). Urbanization, measured by the urban population share, helps in constituting planned infrastructure in place and contributes to protect people from larger local environmental burdens. However, urbanization has also been blamed for climate change and aggravating the impact of prevailing environmental problems. Hence, need of the hour is an eco friendly and sustainable urban planning for balanced and healthy urban development with active involvement of stake holders.

India is amongst the many developing countries witnessing a rapid rural to urban shift. The urban population in India increased from around 27.8% (286 million) in 2001 to 31.2% (377 million) in 2011and is estimated to grow to 40% by 2030 and more than 50% by 2050. (C. Chandramouli and R.General, 2011).

Baneful impacts of Urbanization

Three major problems associated with urbanization in our country have been:

(a) Problems of infrastructure, resulting in serious deterioration in provisions for basic infrastructure and services like water supply, sewerage, drainage, public health and sanitation, roads, transport , education etc. due to their escalating demand. On an average 38 % of the urban population lives below the poverty line and 80 million people live in slums without basic services and amenities. (AIF, Poverty in India, Azad India Foundation, Kishanganj, India).

(b) Problems of governance and management, resulting in inadequate provisions of urban infrastructure and services. Predicament in the delivery of urban services in our country is consequential of neglect of urban planning and infrastructure by state governments, further aggravated by inadequate investment in urban infrastructure assets, poor maintenance of public infrastructure assets, weak administration, poor system of delivery, lack of accountability to the community etc.

(c) Problem of sustainability, including environmental, economic and technological sustainability, generally dominated by environmental impact. Problems of pollution, congestion, deteriorating quality of life and infrastructure and rising cost while competing with each other for jobs, investments, talents etc., coupled with challenges of climate change, resource depletion, alteration in ecological cycle and biodiversity, are the major challenges being faced by the cities. Complexities in the socio- economic systems in the cities and urban areas have increased, experiencing economic turmoil, high rate of urbanization, climatic variations and vast population growth, with sustainability at stake. (Cisco Report, 2013). These factors have hampered growth and cities have become disordered and unorganized (Johnson, 2008).

(d) Problems related to health, traffic pollution, scarcity of resources, waste management and poor infrastructure arise and hence development of city falls apart. (Borja 2007; Marceau 2008; Toppeta 2010). These problems trap the growth of the cities and dismantle it completely (Dawes, Cresswell & Pardo 2009, Rittel&Webber 1973; Weber& Khademian 2008)

These challenges across developing and underdeveloped countries are, to an extent, similar, but their priority may vary with the size in population. Essentially the cities need to become more sustainable, inclusive, livable and efficient, in other words, 'Smart'. Thus the concept of smart city, using technology to address these issues in a smarter way, is one strategy being deployed to efficiently and effectively cope with these present challenges as well as move towards a sustainable future. The purpose of the Smart Cities is to drive economic growth and improve the quality of life of people by enabling local area development, harnessing technology that leads to smart outcomes. Leading smart cities such as Stockholm, Barcelona, New York, Vienna, Toronto etc. have incorporated efficiency into buildings, infrastructure, and social spaces using technological advancements, resulting in increased livability, workability, and sustainability of these places. Inspired by these smart city developments, India is planning to build 100 smart cities in various parts of the country. Mr. Narendra Modi, Honorable Prime Minister of India, in his speech, emphasised, "Cities in the past were built on riverbanks, now they are built along highways. But in the future, they will be built based on availability of optical fiber networks and next-generation infrastructure."

Evolution of the concept Smart City

During the early 1990s, creative ways of urban planning and design began to emerge. In 1992, 'smart growth' emerged as a concept suggesting an alternative paradigm to the urban sprawl, detached housing and dependence on automobiles. This concept gained immense popularity but gradually faded away and a new concept called 'Intelligent Cities' emerged. Intelligent Cities aimed at finding out how data and Information Technology (IT) could impact the way cities function. From the ongoing debates on smart growth and intelligent cities, the idea "smart city" emerged. During the same time, much of the discourses came from 'intelligent' and 'smart' enterprises like IBM, CISCO, Siemens and the Massachusetts Institute of Technology (MIT). Other technology giants like Hitachi and Microsoft also came up with "smart" technologies for cities. [(Townsend, 2014, Harrison, 2011)

Discourses on smart cities gained prominence with the break of global economic crisis in 2008. The period saw extreme cuts in urban finances and social welfare and sought the assistance of private sector to provide public urban services. (Paroutis, Bennett and Heracleous, 2014). Thus emerged a smart city model which assumed that there is a common goal for the city which can be optimized to increase efficiency in different sectors such as transport, health care etc so as to benefit the city as a whole. (Steiner and Veel, 2014). In 2011, the smart city trademark was officially registered to IBM. However, there is also no set definition of smart city as the concepts defining smart cities are still emerging and varies from one place to another depending on the level of development, willingness to change and reform along with resources and aspirations of the city residents. There are an array of conceptual variants such as "Digital City" and "Intelligent City" (Hollands 2008) and therefore use of the label "smart City" has not been consistent. (Chourabi, et al, 2012).

A city can be defined as 'smart' when investments in human and social capital as well as traditional and modern Information and Communications Technology (ICT), infrastructure, fuel, sustainable economic development and high quality of life, with a wise management of natural resources through participatory governance are implemented, having a profound impact on how cities are planned and managed for bettering the quality of life for citizens, provisioning water supply, transportation, entertainment, safety and security, delivery of government services, participatory governance, supportive digital inclusion, intelligent buildings, energy and environment, efficient carbon emission and pollution controlled city development.

Smart Cities Mission in India

Smart Cities Mission (SCM), an ambitious project aiming at enabling the latest smart technology and infrastructure in our cities, is a national initiative by the Ministry of Urban Development (MoUD) to build a foundation for 100 smart cities in five years (2015-16 to 2019-20) (MoUD, "Smart City Mission And Guidelines," 2015). However, the SCM does not incorporate the specific characteristics that need to be included in a 'smart' city. Urban development research points towards two pillars of urban growth, i.e. entrepreneurial environment and quality of life, represented by companies and people, which are significant and necessary for a competitive city to develop (Szczech-Pietkiewicz, E, 2013.). The vision statements for Smart Cities envisioned an eco-friendly, sustainable, inclusive, livable, safe quality of life for its citizens with a vibrant economy encouraging heritage and tourism. These keywords describe city officials' visions for developing their smart cities and reflect the goals to be achieved.

The focus of smart city should be on sustainable and inclusive development that provide core infrastructure and give a decent quality of life to its citizens, exploiting technology for offering more structured and hospitable living conditions for its citizens designing smart physical, social, institutional and economic infrastructure. An approval of Rs 98,000 crores was made for execution of 100 smart cities, along with Atal Mission for Rejuvenation and Urban Transformation (AMRUT), which is an urban rejuvenation programme for 500 towns and cities. (Upadhyaya 2016: 700)

The SCM is the first significant step towards the comprehensive implementation of the smart city concept in India. The MoUD defines a smart city as building and promoting cities that provide core infrastructure and give a decent quality of life to its citizens, a clean and sustainable environment with application of "smart" solutions, building upon existing infrastructural assets and resources, and proposing resource efficient initiatives. The mission has further defined smartness in terms of both physical and non-physical assets such as water supply, waste management, energy sources and supply, safety, citizen participation, economy, employment, and education. The MoUD initiated the SCM through the India Smart Cities Challenge. The Indian cities competed for central government funding to take part in this challenge, by submitting a Smart City Proposal (SCP). On an average, each city selected will receive USD 15.03 million per year from the central government to spend on smart city development. An equal amount of matching funds will be contributed by the State/Urban Local Body (ULB) and therefore, nearly USD 15,031 million of Government and ULB funds will be available for smart city development. (Upadhyaya 2016: 700)

The SCM' s purpose is to drive economic growth and improve the quality of life of people by enabling local area development that has three components : (a) Area-based development (ABD) that will transform existing areas, including slums, by retrofitting and redevelopment thereby improving livability of the whole city; (b) Green-field projects that will develop new areas in the city in order to accommodate the expanding population in urban areas; and (c) Pan-City Development (PAN) that envisages application of selected smart solutions to existing city-wide infrastructure. (Upadhyaya 2016: 702)

As of now, 60 cities (from the list of 100 proposed smart cities) have been shortlisted in the SCM and provided with initial funding for Smart City Proposal (SCP) implementation. The SCM tried to capture citizens' aspirations in terms of priority areas for smart city development, which shows that the major focus is on smart living and mobility. Decades of urban underinvestment have left cities in India with dire deficits in critical domains, including railways, roads, ports, airports, telecommunications, and electricity generation. India ranked 89th out of 142 countries in terms of her infrastructure in the World Economic Forum's Global Competitiveness Report for 2011- 2012. The report criticized

Indian transport, ICT, and energy infrastructure as "largely insufficient and ill-adapted to the needs of the growing population" (Agarwal, 2013). Again, education and health services suffer from poor service delivery, lack of quality choices, and lack of access to expensive privately provided services especially for the poor (Singh,. Badaya et al, 2014:143). The third priority domain based on the citizen survey was environment. The growing population fuels the exploitation of natural resources and creates high levels of pollution, making the environment a priority for a smart city.

Physical Infrastructure

Including cost-efficient and intelligent systems like urban mobility, housing stock energy generation, water supply, sewerage, drainage and sanitation facilities, integrated with technology.

Social Infrastructure

Including quality education, healthcare, entertainment facilities along with performance and creative arts, sports, open spaces, children's parks and gardens, promoting inclusiveness in city for Scheduled Castes, Scheduled Tribes, socially and financially backwards, minorities, disabled and women into the mainstream of development.

Economic Infrastructure

Including development of Incubation Centers, Skill Development Centers, Industrial Parks and Export Processing Zones, Information Technology / Bio Technology Parks, Trade & Service Centers, Financial Centers And Services, Logistics Hub, Warehousing and Freight Terminals, Mentoring and Counseling Services to attract investments and create employment opportunities.

Components of a Smart City

A smart city must provide a basic infrastructure for better quality of life to its citizens, in terms of good quality but affordable housing, 24 x 7 water supply, sanitation, electric supply along with clean air, quality education, safety and security for women, children and the elderly, inclusiveness, entertainment, sports, access to public utilities, cost efficient healthcare, robust and high speed interconnectivity, fast & efficient urban mobility etc. A smart city should be competitive enough to create employment opportunities for every section of the society, should attract investments, experts professionals and people to take up development activities with the ease to do business, as well as transparency, accountability and opportunities for participation in governance.

Smart Water Management

Smart water metering and billing systems can measure water consumption in real time and can automatically communicate this information for monitoring and billing purposes. By combining smart water metering and mobile banking, a reliable transparent and secure flow of funds and information between the consumer and water service provider can be achieved. Mapping of water resources and distribution is possible with Geographic Information System (GIS) techniques. GIS-based mapping integrated with the hydraulic modeling, metering with analyzers and online billing systems, improved water availability due to monitoring of input and output points and checking of water distribution losses with smart sensors in water taps, thereby eliminating useless flow of water when there is no body to use it, should be implemented.

Waste water Integration and automation of water treatment plant and sewerage systems, Enterprise resource planning (Oracle) system, generation of database for sewerage services and grievance management services, funded under state projects and other local bodies, are likely to improve service delivery, bill collection and procurement, leading to efficiency and transparency in waste water sector.

Smart Transportation and Traffic Management Systems

Understanding the flow and congestion of vehicular traffic is essential for efficient road systems in cities. Smooth vehicle flows reduce journey times, reduce emissions and save energy. Monitoring traffic, whether road vehicles or people, is useful for operators of roads and transport hubs. The monitoring system calculates the average speed of the vehicles, which transit over a roadway by taking the time mark at two different points. Wireless vehicle detector based on magnetic induction technology and wireless communication technology can collect data of traffic flow, speed of vehicle, occupancy ratio and moving direction, providing these to system integrator for smooth traffic management. Other options including car sharing, use of non-motorized vehicle or pedestrian ways can make a transport system smart. These advance applications aim to provide innovative services relating to different modes of transport and traffic management and enable various users to be aware with safe, more coordinated and smarter approach to use transport networks.

Smart Street Lighting

Intelligent street lighting refers to public street lighting that adapts to the movement by pedestrians, cyclists and cars, dimming when there is no activity, but brightening in case of any movement. These smart streetlights become energy efficient when combined with renewable energy techniques. Advanced street light system of energy efficient lighting combined with LED lighting, vertical axis wind turbines and solar photovoltaic, street lighting with motion sensor are a few examples which will automatically be switched on when there is some movement.

Smart Health

Technologies can immensely help those who treat our illnesses, heal our injuries and find ways to battle our diseases even better. It can also help healthy individuals to make smarter choices about their health care. Smart Health Systems are able to sense and diagnose complex situations. Digital interactive technologies like touch screen displays enable fast access to digital information, to view, discuss, modify and save in real time. Access to immediate digital information, can enable easy view for status of beds and patients and new information to add as soon as changes happen, resulting in more simple patient management. The recording of patient admissions, discharges, and transfers are instant and can be easily discussed, drawn and noted upon, and distributed externally, via email, , if required.

Smart Education

With growing urbanization, cities need to be a center of learning to make everybody smarter for skill upgradation and capacity building. Preparing today's students for life in the increasingly complex and technological world of the future is the need of the hour. Smart schools can play an important role in improving the physical performance of the city. Intelligent systems can help schools, colleges and universities manage their energy systems, security, communication, and transportation much better by helping to connect departments and campuses in higher education, enabling virtual and online learning, engaging social media and collaborating with contemporary education to change the way children learn. It also enables schools to stay up-to-date with current and timely information, and to leverage teaching resources across schools, campuses, districts and across the world.

Smart Security System

New smart systems can provide innovative connectivity to house even from faraway places during travel activities owing to business travel, children's school schedules and social activities. Remote arm and disarm the security system, easily automate lights or change them remotely before arrival, adjust the thermostat to help save on utility bills or to have a comfortable environment to greet the occupants, access appliances like the coffeemaker or set schedules to automate them, set up the system to get notifications through email, text, phone or real-time video clips of alarms, receive email or text message of selected events, view stored video clips of events from monitored areas of the home etc are components of smart security system.

Smart Information and Communications Technology (ICT)

Information technology is an umbrella term that includes communication device, applications and various services associated with it. Progress in information technology is the driving force behind economic growth and a key component of the investments allocated by the governments to build smart cities, to improve the quality of life of its citizens by providing citizen services over communication networks involving citizen engagement and job creation. Information and Communications Technology (ICT) reshapes and integrates world's economies, governments and societies. In developing countries like India, all the stakeholders in a city including government officials, private business entities and public are in process to exploit ICT for making efficient services, boost financial status and build up community association. Innumerable problems can be avoided, anticipated and mitigated by analyzing huge data available. (Bakici, Almirall & Wareham, 2013). . Smart cities must exploit information and communication technology to increase sustainability and improve quality of life for the citizens. However, availability of technologically sound human resource with practical skills and educating and training these employees with IT skills can be a major challenge.

Sustainability

Sustainability may be defined as bringing about economic and social development without disrupting the environment. Sustainable development today is not a choice but a pre-condition for development. With the advent of energy efficient technology, a harmonious marriage between development and environment is possible. It is time that each one of us adopt an 'energy-efficient and green' mind-set and use the natural resources available equitably, judiciously and save them for our future generations, as the best way to predict future is to create it. The major requirements of city environments comprise of sustaining water, energy, and food supplies, managing waste and reducing greenhouse gas emission. Cities consume 75% of our energy resources, and emit 80% of the carbon that is harming our environment (Charbel 2013). To diminish the impact of cities on the environment resource, it is vital to encourage an effective and intelligent deployment of technology, integrate infrastructures, increase the resilience of cities to environmental shocks by providing an enhanced quality of life and decreasing its carbon footprint. Setting a smart city vision and effectively moving towards it, with a systems-based approach, is imperative to ensure optimum resource efficiency and security, along with preserving socially inclusive growth.

Smart Governance

Governance is a major execution challenge for smart cites. Smart governance ensures efficient communication and integral connection between the government and public for efficient delivery of services and information sharing, enhancing capacity of governance by improving the way of resolving issues faced by public and timely response to the feedbacks, complaints and suggestion in a professional manner. A move to digital or e-governance is essential for an effective and efficient administration of the smart cities. Smart Governance includes political and active citizen participation, citizen services and the smart use of e-Government. (Gil-Garcia & Pardo 2005). E-government can be explained as an initiative to improve the decision making process, improve public policy-making and improve public governance with ICT, allowing the citizens to involve comprehensively in all these aspects. Internet is the most widely used channel of communication for most people and ICT can enhance democratic processes and increase opportunities for individuals and communities to interact with the government. Smart governance is an important characteristic of a smart city that is based on citizen participation (Giffinger, Fertner, Kramar, Kalasek, Pichler-Milanovic & Meijers, 2007) and private/public partnerships. Smart governance relies on the implementation of smart governance infrastructure that facilitates service integration, collaboration, communication and data exchange (Odendaal, 2003). In this process all the stakeholders including government, public and other private entities are involved to get benefit with the help of efficient communication network for implementing reforms and decision making for future smart cities.

Smart Waste Management

A critical problem faced by most urban areas include lack of an efficient and well maintained sanitation and waste treatment system, leading to various environmental and health hazards. Rapid urbanization and changing lifestyle and food habits have resulted in deposition of increased amount of municipal solid. Dumpsites in almost all cities are handling more waste than capacity, and finding new landfills near cities is almost impossible. Most dumpsites lack systems for leachate collection, landfill gas collection or monitoring, etc. resulting in ground and surface water contamination from runoff, air pollution caused by fires, toxic gases, odour, and public health problems due to mosquitoes and other epidemics. Efforts to reduce waste and environmental pollution, generating renewable energy, and to free up land from using it for landfill is essential. Off-site Real Time Monitoring (OSRT) System, GIS and Global Positioning System (GPS) enabled services, biometric attendance systems for sanitary workers, sensor based applications for smart solid waste management services have shown commendable results in monitoring cleanliness of bins, workforce efficiency and transparency through websites, making data available to the public. Automated Waste Collection System (AWCS) can take care of the conventional methods like door-to-door, curbside, block; community bins collections and transportation to transfer station.

Smart Municipal Services

Integration of all operations of municipal corporation through Geographic Information System (GIS), computerized building plan scrutiny and approvals, standardized online citizen administration, traffic information system and many others as some of the smart governance initiatives undertaken by urban local bodies, accelerating the pace of development. Municipal e-revenue systems using GIS linked property database, Tulana, an online application for service level benchmarking, initiated by the Karnataka Municipal Administration, E-tendering, Dynamic Integration of Property Registration and Land Records

Administration System, Comprehensive Public Works Management Information and Management system for Public Works Department (State level) and many more advanced applications, catering to the smart service delivery in this sector have been in initiated. Tax administration improved to a large extent as a result of augmentation of municipal revenues for financing and maintenance of municipal services and infrastructure with focus on reforms in property tax using GIS, integrated with property database systems. Submission of tenders, documents, Earnest Money Deposit (EMD), security deposits, tenders integrated with the accounting and ICT enabled services led to speed-up in service delivery of infrastructure through e-tendering and related smart services.

Vibrant Economy

Economy is one of the major drivers of smart city initiatives. A key indicator to measure growing city competition is the ability of the city as an economic engine (Giffinger, Kramar, & Haindl, 2007). A smart economy includes all around economic competitiveness such as entrepreneurship, trademarks, innovation, productivity and flexibility of the labour market and integration in the national and global market. What truly makes a city intelligent and smart are constant economic growth and maximization of profits, facilitating the flow of capital. Creating an environment for industrial actions and business development is pivotal to a smart city (Bronstein, 2009) The economic outcomes of the smart city initiatives are business creation, job creation, workforce development, and improvement in the productivity.

Legal Compliance

Well-laid principles and guidelines, governing the smart cities, are important for efficient and smooth working between administration and local public bodies. Innovative policies facilitating both technical and non-technical requirements for urban growth are essential. Therefore, commensurate policies that support the development of smart cities must be formulated by the governments and the organizing entities (Eger & Maggipinto, 2010).

Conclusion

Making cities smart will take time and effort. It is necessary to create an enabling policy and regulatory environment. A study conducted by the Center for Study of Science, Technology and Policy, September 2015 recommends the following action points in order to facilitate the building of a robust Smart City Reference Framework, which includes creating a catalogued platform for smart city knowledge resources, accessible by all, making a way towards informed deliberation and helping academics, think tanks and corporate agencies to identify relevant research areas, bringing together the ongoing efforts on relevant research, ensuring mechanisms of convergence with various other related programmes and projects, paving way for a coherent and consistent process for strategic urban planning, along with an assessment of smart city planning and regulatory framework with constitution of an expert group on Smart Cities at the National level, supplemented by expert groups at the state level. Involving different government departments from the initial stages of this activity will instill a sense of ownership in the stakeholder departments and will ease the process of implementation at later stages.

Our cities have a great potential to become a smart city provided it is equipped with provision of adequate infrastructure, conservation of resources and inclusive development with government-people-private participation. The challenge before the government is to build inclusive smart cities for all its residents, irrespective of whether they are rich or poor. In a country like India, the process of making a city smart should be people centric. The ability for all citizens to communicate with one another and agencies and groups that represent them provides a new sense of possibility to the idea that smart cities are based on smart communities whose citizens can play an active part in their design.

References

Agarwal M (2013), "The Opportunity and Challenge of India's Infrastructure," Source: https://www.pwc.com/gx/en/capital-projects-infrastructure/assets/gridlines-india-article-2013.pdf, accessed on 01.05.2020.

AIF, Poverty in India, Azad India Foundation, Kishanganj, India, Source: http://www.azadindia.org/social-issues/poverty-in-india/html), accessed on 01.05.2020.

Bakici, T., Almirall, E., & Wareham J (2013), "A Smart City Initiative: The Case of Barcelona", *Journal of the Knowledge Economy*, 4(2), pp.135-148.

Borja, J (2007), "Counterpoint: Intelligent Cities And Innovative Cities", Universitat Oberta de Catalunya (UOC) Papers: E-Journal on the Knowledge Society, Source: http://www.uoc.edu/uocpapers/5/dt/eng/mitchell.pdf, accessed on 01.05.2020.

Bronstein, Z (2009), "Industry and The Smart City", *Dissent*, 56(3), pp. 27-34. Available from http://www.community-wealth.org/_pdfs/articlespublications/cross-sectoral/article-bronstein.pdf, accessed on 01.05.2020.

Chandramouli C. and.General R (2011.), "Census of India 2011, *Provisionals Population Totals,* New Delhi, Government of India.

Charbel A (2013), "The Smart City Cornerstone: Urban Efficiency", http://www.digital21. gov.hk/eng/relatedDoc/download/2013/079%20SchneiderElectric%20(Annex).pdf, accessed on 01.05.2020.

Chourabi H.et al (2012), "Understanding Smart Cities: An Integrative Framework", *45th Hwaii International Conference on System Sciences,* Maui, HI, doi: 10.1109/HICSS.2012.615, accessed on 01.05.2020.

Cisco Report (2013), "Smart Cities and Internet of Everything-The Foundation for Delivering Next-Generation Citizen Services", sponsored by Cisco, Source: https://www.cisco.com/web/strategy/docs/scc/ioe_citizen_ svcs_white_ paper_idc_ 2013.pdf. accessed on 01.05.2020.

Dawes, S. S, Cresswell, A. M. and Pardo, T. A (2009), "From "Need To Know" To "Need To Share": Tangled Problems, Information Boundaries, And The Building Of Public Sector Knowledge Networks", *Public Administration Review,* 69(3), pp.392-402.

Eger, J. M., & Maggipinto, A (2010), "Technology as a Tool Of Transformation: E-Cities and The Rule Of Law" in A. D'Atri & Saccà, D. (eds.), *Information Systems: People, Organizations, Institutions, and Technologies;* Berlin/Heidelberg, Germany: Physica- Verlag, pp. 23-30.

Giffinger R., Fertner C., Kramar H., Kalasek R., Pichler-Milanoviü N. & Meijers E (2007), "Smart Cities: Ranking of European Medium-Sized Cities. Vienna", Austria: Centre of Regional Science (SRF), Vienna University of Technology. Available from http://www.smartcities.eu/download/smart_cities_final_report.pdf. , accessed on 01.05.2020.

Gil-García, J. R., and Pardo, T. A (2005), "E-Government Success Factors: Mapping Practical Tools to Theoretical Foundations", *Government Information Quarterly,* 22(2), pp.187-216.

Harrison, C and Donnelly, I. A (2011), "A Theory of Smart Cities", in proceedings of the 55th Annual Meeting of the ISSS-2011, Hull, UK, 55(1).

Hollands, R.G. (2008), "Will The Real Smart City Please Stand Up?" *City,* 12(3), pp.303-320.

Johnson, B (2008), Cities, "Systems of Innovation and Economic Development", *Innovation: Management, Policy & Practice*, 10(2-3), pp.146-155.

Marceau, J (2008), "Introduction: Innovation in the City and Innovative Cities", *Innovation: Management, Policy & Practice*, 10(2-3), pp.136-145.

Mauher, M. and Smokvina, V(2006), "Digital To Intelligent Local Government Transition Framework", in proceedings of the 29th International Convention of MIPRO, Opatija, Croatia, May 22-26. Available from http://www. mmcconsul tinghr/Download/2008/03/07/Mauher_M_ Digital_ to_Intelligent_City_Transition_Framework.pdf, accessed on 01.05.2020.

MoUD (2015), Smart City Mission and Guidelines.

Odendaal, N (2003), "Information and Communication Technology and Local Governance: Understanding The Difference Between Cities in Developed and Emerging Economies", *Computers, Environment and Urban Systems* 27(6), pp.585-607.

Paroutis S, Bennett M and Heracleous L (2014), "A Strategic View on Smart City Technology: The Case of IBM Smarter Cities During A Recession", *Technological Forecasting and Social Change,* Vol. 89, pp. 262-272.

Rittel, H. W. J., & Webber, M (973), "Dilemmas In A General Theory of Planning", *Policy Sciences*, 4(2), June, pp. 155-169.

Steiner H and Veel K (2014), "For the Smarter Good of Cities: On Cities, Complexity and Slippages in the Smart City Discourse", in Stamatina Th and Rassia Panos M. Pardalos(ed.), *Cities for Smart Environmental and Energy Futures,* Springer, Berlin, Heidelberg.

Szczech-Pietkiewicz, E (2013), "Poland's Urban Competitiveness in the European Context", *The Polish Review*, University of Illinois Press, 58(2), pp. 15-36.

Singh S, Badaya S. et al (2014), "Health Care In Rural India: A Lack Between Need And Feed," *South Asian Journal Of Cancer*, 3(2), p. 143.

Toppeta, D (2010), The Smart City Vision: How Innovation and ICT Can Build Smart, "Livable", Sustainable Cities. The Innovation Knowledge Foundation. Source: http://www.thinkinnovation.org/file/research/23/en/Toppeta_Report_005_2010.pdf, accessed on 01.05.2020.

Townsend, A. M. (2014). *Smart Cities: Big Data, Civic Hackers, And The Quest For A New Utopia*. New York, NY: W. W. Norton & Company. [Google Scholar]

United Nations. Department of Economic and Social Affairs, Population Division: World Urbanization Prospects, the 2014 revision: Highlights," 2015.

Upadhyaya V (2016), "Smart Cities: A Vision for Development of Indian Cities", *Imperial Journal of Interdisciplinary Research*, 2(10), http://www.onlinejournal.in, accessed on 01.05.2020.

Weber, E. P. and Khademian, A. M (2008) "Wicked Problems, Knowledge Challenges, And Collaborative Capacity Builders in Network Settings", *Public Administration Review,*; 68(2), pp.334 349.

Chapter 3

Neo-Liberal Families and Contemporary Urban Culture

Maitreyee Bardhan Roy and Subir Kumar Bardhan Roy

Introduction

While concentrating on `Neo Liberal families, in India, the researchers try to focus on the 21st century young generation`s perception of family under neo-liberalist socio-economic structure prevalent in the Indianurban culture with specific reference to the family as a fundamental socio-cultural construct. The chief feature of neo liberal family is to challenge Indian patriarchal family structure existing in Indian urban scenario during the 19th and the 20th century. Increasingly, the financial contribution of both genders has ensured the equal voice of the bother on the significant family issues. However, the main perception of the study grants greater prominence to women, especially as mother as she plays by far the most important role during the format years. Similarly, the change in family culture is examined from the children`s perspective since it is indicative of future trends in the family, society and by extension, the nation. Since the Neo liberal families are a recent phenomenon in the present day Indian society ,the author of the article tries to focus on the Indian Neo-liberal family structure that involves varieties of the family patterns presently observed in the city culture in India. On the whole, the traditional family patterns are also equally important in the country having 121 million population

In the Indian socio –cultural context, the concept neo-liberal families indicate radical family trends and both the men and the women have equal contribution towards the change. However before understanding the concept Neo-Liberalism from the Indian urban family contest its essential to understand the concept of 'family' from the traditional perspective. As per the traditionalists understanding, the term family refers to the association of husband, wife and children as the prime members but the neo liberalists fail to limit the family by imposing a barricade on that. They, on the contrary, refer to the association of two persons (neo-family), going beyond gender stratification. Considering the contending ideologies associated with the terminology , the present paper tries to concentrate on the 21st century`s concept of family where individuals are evolving on their own orbit ,wherein mother / father or the overall existence of families are dwindling under bye-sexual or unisexual equation. The researcher in the article focuses on the effect of neo-liberalism more on the families than on the societies in the post modem era.

The Shift in `The Family Ethos` in 21stCentury India

Indian sociologists, while commenting on the term ` family, regard it as a unit that include father, mother, sons, their wives, unwedded daughters and grandchildren. The definition of family thus included all staying under one roof and thriving under the umbrella of the family head for their daily bread. The term family as such refers to certain obligatory customs which are to be followed by all staying under the same roof and following the rules of family head. The definition of the term family has been officially rectified first by the Section 2 of CCS (CONDUCT) Rule 1964. Accordingly, the family members of Government Servants, include spouse, dependent sons and daughters including step children or `any other dependent person` related to them or their spouse by blood or by marriage. (Times of India July 22, 2016) The official recognition of the term `any other dependent persons` re-establishes the position of village inmates residing in the urban families as the dependent. The term `Family 'thus reconfirms the vastness of the relation web in Indian society. Although the changing pattern of the families are recorded with the changing needs of the time. The existence of the same in its traditional form receives cognizance by modern authors (Henrica, Donner 2015) in their writings. They have recorded the changes in the middle class family pattern by referring to how the concept of home continues to be mediated through the joint family ideal and patri-locality by recognizing the daughters ` property right as well as the right to stay under same roof sharing all happiness and sorrows together. The term 'Family' indicates the household ménage that solely include dependents only. To differentiate Indian urban families from the European concept, reference may be made to `The Collins English Dictionary`. It defines `family` as a group of people related to each other especially parents and their children`. While in the Oxford Dictionary` the term `Family` is defined in much more detail. It is defined as a social group consisting of parents and their offspring. The principal function of the head of the family is to make provisions for all its members. The present research, aims to concentrate on the changing trends in Indian families with the changes in the parlance from the traditional Family to ` Neo Liberal Family` The concept, "neo-liberal family' gained popularity in the post Globalization era because of the impact of neo-liberal capitalism which` has extended its control over the younger generation in Urban India, especially in the `city` family culture. The researcher, while focusing on the family journey in India from joint family to the Neo Liberal family the author tries to focus on the new socio-economic trends which influence its formation. Since the term family and children are traditionally closely intertwined, the author of the article while raising the issues relating to the families, tries to look into the diversified family pattern in Kolkata metropolis to analyze the new generation families and its effect on children.

Indian Family and its correlation with the Socio-Political Setup

Though the family is a micro –social unit , the influence of State politico social set up have been influencing the family so intensely that family structure also changes with the shift of the political system of the country .Hence ,the 18th century feudalism or colonial culture had been so ingrained to the social structure that the traces of the same were reflected in the family culture through land lord system with string class structure in the society and its most micro unit the family also carried with it the ethos through joint family structure with a dominant family head nurturing the everybody under one roof. For the same reason the families in India were looked upon as a unit that not only included husband wife and children. It was looked upon as a social unit but it was treated as an association of family relatives, dependents` family all brothers their families and the unwedded sisters, with house hold helpers helping the family activities included under the parlance `family` To speak in a more specific way, we can say that the head of the family was not at all aware of the number of people residing in the house and in what capacity they stayed in the house. But he never refused to help them out by offering them their daily sustenance. So, in a way, the family may be looked up as a small form of village, where all inmates have the right to, live and eat together. Similarly, 19th century individualism had its reflection in Indian families and gave birth to an elitist community; who through the adoption of the culture of an elitist system started looking for its own interest. They came to be known as the `Babu or the elite ` . They spent their days in pomp and splendor and were oblivious of the plight of the community at large. Historically, it is contended that this group of families or the Babus have been responsible for the breakdown of the socio-economic structure, The Babu` families of Bengal were also banished following the breakdown of individualism. The 20th century parliamentary democracy during post independent India promoted the democratic system associated with the welfare state and the reflection of the same was expressed through extended family system in India. Considering the shift in family structure in concurrence with the socio-political stature of the society, the same trend the neo-liberal family structure is the outcome of Globalization and Liberalization in the 21st century.

Family Journey from Liberalism to Neo Liberalism: The family journey from liberalism to Neo liberalism, a natural outcome of social evolution in the West, is considered one of the most recent trends that has molded contemporary urban culture in India. Therefore, Neo-liberal families are merely a jargon to the average Indian middle-class families. The intrusion of neo-liberalist culture in Indian society has caused a cultural shock to the common masses, especially the older generation (among the middle-class traditional families). The academic knowledge of the educated class have enabled them to differentiate it from the previous socio-political orders such as European Individualism of the 18thand the 19th century which was replaced by Liberalism in the 20th century with its welfare concept .The failure of welfare theory and the economic crisis all over Europe in 1970s and 1980s and again in 2007(21st century) made space for the resurgence of Individualism in new disguise namely Neo-Liberalism and automatically the influence of the same gave birth to the Neo-liberal family structure in India during the 21st century. The sudden shift of family culture could never be predicted by the common masses. The cultural shock among the middle-class families took some time to ingest, tolerate and subsequently accept the changes. This was common in the earlier phases of family changes too. Thus, the few of them who come forward to carry the banner had to face the consequences of hostile resistance to change. Closed community boycott and non-cooperation from the community are the common form of resistance that rebels come to the concerned person refusing traditional system. Hence those who have been practicing that culture remain aware and stay mentally prepared to face the same consequences. However , the figure is so insignificant at its initial stage that the close community boycott does not make much difference to the society but with the growing popularity of visual publicity media, the cases when highlighted in the public ,the reaction against such practices starts but the adoption of the practice among the media personalities, the acceptance of the same become easier to the community as a whole and with the change of time the practice is accepted and adored to the society or the societal reaction becomes cold and are looked up the stray cases in the city culture .However ,in regard to neo families concept, a third factor has been involved as its longstanding effect and are expected to create an ever-lasting reaction to the society .It is because the outcome of the neo-liberal families are so intense to the children that are born to the society with the absence of a regular identity of a full -fledged family fail to overcome psycho-social anxiety crisis or attention crisis ,that develop s on him for being the absence of any one of the family members leading to an increase in inquisitiveness among the peer group to raise questions on incompleteness in the family .The question who is responsible for that, the family, the society or the parents create an apathy of the child towards the people around him Hence, the unresolved question is left unanswered to them make them more and more apathetic feeling towards the society The Kolkata society is moving towards the phase as a result suicide among teen ager, crime in them ,criminal assaults are increasing in number.

To the Indian scholars, Individualism or Neo- Liberalism were dealt with as the two ideological jargons whose application at the micro stage and it families become so intense that under the existing socio-cultural structure its instant assimilation with the Indian traditional society is difficult to predict. The whole socio-cultural scenario is under consistent pressure and the overall scenario became different with the upcoming of Globalization in 1990s and its accompanying concept ,.The Neo-Liberalism in the 21st century though started spreading up in Indian socio-cultural stratum in the end of twentieth century, the Globalization paved the way to the entry to Neo-Liberalism in the Indian family culture in the same pace as that of 17th century feudalism had impacted the land lord family system under the feudal regime and the `Family with its aristocratic outfit indicated the selfish change of the Landlords families in India where the management of the affairs of the community had been taken up by them as their responsibility. They captured an important position in nurturing the community or the villages falling under their territorial regime. Thus, the meaning of the term family in India during the 17th century indicated a huge population sharing the same housing or the same roof. The Land Lord and his people (close relative or distant relatives and also the home domestics) Thus the term family in the 17th century was not confined to husband wife and children only`. The upcoming of English classical philosophy , while speaking of the entry of individualistic ideologies in the Europe ,they could not even imagine that the influence of the same had influenced the micro stage social structure i.e. the family. The family culture, back in India, thus, was influenced by the babu culture (gentleman culture) allowed the liberalists to enter into and to settle down in the life of few upper-class minority population in the same manner as the individualism did through the spreading up of its culture in the 18th and some part of the 19th century. Interestingly, the reverse effect the same was reflected under the Babu culture too. The Baboos could not last for a longer period of time in Indian family system (the extravagant living style of the Babus or the aristocrats ultimately resulted in anarchism in the family style of living and many land Lords` family had lost their properties due to their elitist style of living. The adoption of Parliamentary democracy in India ended up the land Lord or the Zamindari system and consecutively, the system of extended families with the welfare customs lost its entity from the Indian metropolitan culture. Thus the year1947 marked the independence of India and with the establishment of Democratic Republic in the country and with the partition of Bengal the joint family system almost ended up and the extended family structure with the welfare concept came into being but the partition of Bengal compelled the migrant population to end up their extended family structure too .Thus when the reflection of state politico social scenario had been influencing the culture of the people ,the upcoming of neo-liberal family structure became inevitable with the upcoming of globalization and liberalization in 1990`s. Globalization thus made space for neo- Individualism with the neo-liberal outfit. It started intermingling with in Indian families with urban culture by spreading its hegemony over the traditional Indian culture and captured a dominant position on the young generation working masses in India. The present article while evaluating the effect of Neo-liberalism on ` the new generation Indians 'will make an effort to focus on the history of the development of neo liberalism in the modern Indian family system prevailing over the traditional family system in India.

Definition of Neo-Liberal Families in India

Neo-liberalism if argued as the 20th century resurgence of 18and the 19th century laissez-faire concept, there remains no scope for offering it a special attention .Hence , Neo-Liberalism demanded a special attention to the dictionary of the western scholars originally in 1938 and its long standing effect in 1970s and 1980s, the growing financial scarcity, encouraged the further revival of neo-liberalism or Individualism in the west and ultimately economic crisis of 2007-08 gave leverage to the people of the west to practice individualistic philosophy in life. The advocates of Free Market policies though successfully avoided the use of the term "neoliberal" but with the growing importance of economic philosophy in Europe ,the usage "neoliberal" as nurtured in Europe encouraged the reintroduction of the same in the Western world in 1980s. (Augusto Pinochet's economic reforms in the form of Neo-Liberalism adopted in Chile in 1980s and in India the neo-liberal society started spreading up to the social fabric of the country holding the hands of Globalization and Liberalization in 1990s due to the country`s low economic management system (under the regime of then Prime Minister of India, Rajiv Gandhi, the inevitability of IMF loan by the Government of the country brought in the pressure for policy imposition in India, and the country, as an obligation to the IMF loan was compelled to become a part of the Washington Consensus. The neo-economic policy encouraged Globalization on the one hand and on the other hand imposed the policies of open door to India.)

The Neo-liberalists ideology not only promoted individualism in the socio-cultural milieu in India ,the new generation intellectual class by making a space for their unique style of living encouraged the development of a new social order and its everlasting impact gave birth to the neo-family culture that gave birth to a new face to the existing family structure in India .The varieties of family structure that started showing face under the neo family structure in the Indian city life included ; 1. Nuclear family with working couple (Children brought up with Surrogate mothers (Ayas or Other Mothers) 2. Husband -wife residing in two different homes (childless or with child in the same form as in point No.1) for employment needs 3.Same Sex families 4 Live in families, 5LGBTE families.6. Single mother or single father families 7. ARTS children families and 8 the families nurturing Biogenic culture. Since all these factors could not uproot the traditional culture from the traditional middleclass families, they still continued to dominate side by side with the neo-liberal culture. Considering the existence of both the system at a time, the field survey included those neo-liberalist groups under discussion. The traditional families interrogated in the present study as such marked the existence of multidimensional family structure as was existing under the Indian social-cultural scenario. Interestingly, the traditional extended families persisted side by side for the safety and security of the children for the protection of the mother/father opted for the diversified family structure. The situation of the traditional families within the modern structure (Bardhan Roy 2020) is also an important look out of the present study. Kolkata city bears the legacy of the existence of working mothers of 1990s (pre-Globalization era) located in the extended families withstanding silent mental torture of the family women for being out of the house for the day. Those semi traditional mothers came forward to support their offspring daughters and daughters-in-law either sharing with them the same house or in a separate house but offering shelter to the grand children during the day .They offer , a significant switch off from the traditional family rules and regulations prevalent in the traditional family culture in Kolkata city ..Hence , the return to the family and stay together for social security stands in front of the queue under the deviated family structure in Neo-liberalist era.

Discussion

In the present article the author proposes six different categories of families brought under two broad classifications i.e. Traditional family and Deviated families. To the first group the term Family indicated the association of people of the two sexes decided to stay together with the willingness to constitute a family and the children born to the association of the two are considered to have been located in the traditional family structure. Even, the husband wife residing in two separate cities for employment needs also fall under the same category. The deviated families include single mother or single father families, Same sex families, LGBTE families, live-in families etc. Under, the neo liberal social structure all the above-mentioned families are legally recognized and all the varieties of families are also visible in all the metropolises if not in large number but their increasing trends could not be ignored under the contemporary urban culture. In Kolkata the single-mother families are many (the single mother family by choice). The researcher has interrogated four such families for information sharing purposes for the present study All the three are divorcee mothers but they opted ARTS Method for the child birth. Two of them stay with the mother`s family and two opted to stay alone. While single father families could not be traced out at the time of the article writing because one father, who made an official announcement of being a single father from Salt Lake City in Kolkata is a very recent case of single fatherhood in the city. However, the first single father in India was also from Kolkata metropolis and historically speaking he is the first Dad of a child. However, in between 2005-2020, the efforts made by two to three persons to be the single father of their children and to nurture them single handedly but lack of social cooperation on the issue and the absence of willingness of ,the surrogate mothers the project failed .Under the patriarchic social structure ,since the child care issues go hand in hand with the women, the concept of single father is still looked up as an elitist culture and it is marked as a highly capitalist order and its manifestation remains in the hands of very rich classes in the society. It is because the elitist socio-cultural background enables them to keep highly trained Governess for the care of the child The suspected social constraint, if not the social evil associated with the culture of the society prohibits a single father as a socially unacceptable precise. The society has to wait for the inflicted change and very soon the same culture is expected to penetrate within the middle-class society too. Hence, the shift of priorities in human relations is expected to ignore the social compulsions in human life, like philosophy of marriage, community living arrangements, the husband-wife relations of mutual respect responsibility of child bearing and rearing the child etc. The new generation Indian promote live-in relations, priority to individual beliefs and the like. The authors of the article, while focusing on the modern perception of life prefers to class it a `Neo-normal families of the twenty-first century`. To the author of the article, Indians residing under neo-liberalist belief, tries to analyze the effect of the changed concept from the individualist point of view .The outcome of the same results in the development of deviated families ,like the same sex families (legally recognized in India).Under LGBTQ, the other manifestation of human nature , legally accepted on 6th September 2018, the Supreme Court of India originally discriminated homosexuality by declaring Section 377 of the Indian Penal Code as unconstitutional because it criminalized consensual between the adult of the same sex. Gay, Bisexual Transgender Queer community. However, on 24th August 2017 neoliberal Indian society has been allowed to express their opinion freely. Their sexual orientation under the right to privacy law allowed them to practice the same as according to their own wishes. Though lesbianism and homosexuality were originally ingrained in Indian culture, and during the colonial era, the Gay sex was declared illegal. Trans-genders, known as Hijras in India and as eunuchs in South East Asia, also they are also known as the transgender people and they had been pushed to performing a specific role in India. They had been living a life of poverty because they are not included in the main stream society. In South-East Asian Nations, the transgender communities are though allowed assimilation, the same is not accepted in India because the Hijra community has been looked up as an exception in South Asian Nations, because they have been isolated from the main stream society and not allowed education and therefore they are left without occupation.

Thus, the situation does not look normal yet. The legal support system has not yet allowed them to help them to easily assimilate them in the society. The expression of the same became evident by the confession of a city transgender Principal, "I have always been addressed as Madam in the College. How can there be any confusion regarding my Gender after so many years? How is it that the District Magistrate –who is the administrator of the College doesn't know my gender?" Says Manbi Bandapadhayay, a Principal if a College to the news print media. 'Times of India',3rd July 2019. This statement of a transgender lady occupying such an important position under the State Government easily becomes the victim of the misconception about her gender, the common masses involved in such sex orientation has to fight the consequences unless the society fails to accept the change in reality. However, the incidence is an unique example of the changed outlook of our traditional society as a manifestation of neo-liberalism or individualism, By neo-liberal family.

Impact of Neo Liberal families in India

The family pattern in modern India under globalization bears a mark of scattered social settings, where diversities in the family patterns are observed side by side with the traditional family structure. The outcome of the same finds expression through social adversities like depression, crime, persistent mutual disrespect among the partners, refusal to take social responsibility, Creating pressure for dowry, Bigamy relation, family conflict, indifference about the partner. The net result of the same are reflected in the families as a whole. The manifestation of the same finds expression in reducing number of children in educated middle class neo- families in India. Though the neo-liberal families group offers avenues for high breed children with higher possibilities in the digitalization era. The important manifestation of the neo-liberal families are diverse and the author of the article prefers to comment on the issues categorically ,so that possible solution to the situation could be urged from the society ,

The world economy may not be able to survive the sudden and horrendous impact of the pandemic on neo-liberal capitalism and may be compelled to formulate innovative economic theories However, the emerging trends suggest that neo-liberal families will flourish in the digital world. There is consensus that while neo-liberals face discrimination and violence in traditional spaces and platforms, they encounter toleration and acceptance in on-line forums. They find connection, validation and advice. Remote control encourages individualism and release from traditional family constraints. In conclusion, there is urgent need to formulate a national education policy that emphasizes the study of our historical and cultural roots so that we do not blindly mimic other nations and make efforts to strengthen community life .

End note

1. The term ` family` in India also indicated a changing trend from a village community (joint family) to an extended family structure to nuclear family and then to the neo family trend under Globalization, the present article makes an effort to record the stage-wise changing pattern of the families with the changing needs of the time .Interestingly, the traditional family structure with its varieties of characteristics were though traced out easily in Indian families in its different forms,the study aims to concentrate on those families to record the changes in the behavioral pattern of the children growing up in neo-liberal family surroundings. In the 21st century the term family indicated something beyond that too. This shift in the concept Family from the association of husband wife and children, to a `Neo-Liberal family` with no set pattern, the present paper aims to record this drastic change in the family pattern in India from a set socio-cultural back drop to a non-set social association,by focusing more on its effect on children and then

to the society as a whole .Since the targeted area of study is confined to West Bengal ,the discussion in the article will be confined to different types of neo-families existing un urban Kolkata by keeping an eye on the traditional families existing in parallel to the neo family structure in Kolkata Metropolis in India.

Reference

Donner H (2013); Being Middle Class in India: A Way of Life. Rutledge.

Gane N (2013). The emergence of Neoliberalism . Thinking through and beyond Michel Foucault`s lectures on bio politics Theory Culture and Society 31(4)3-27.

Henrica Donner (20150) Daughters are just like sons now`: negotiating kin work and property regimes in Kolkata Middle Class families Journal of South Asian Development. Sage Journal

Ibid Sociologyand Neoliberalism-A missing History. Sociology 48(1)DOI 10.1177/0038038513512728

Neoliberalism: A Bibliographic Review: William Devies Goldsmiths university iof London. Theory, Culture and Society 2014 Volume 31(7/8) pp 309-317 SAGE publication0u

Oliva Petter(2019) : Cohabiting couples fastest-growing family type a reporting of The Independent ,published by Times of India ,Kolkata 10th August 201

Chapter 4

India's Urban Sustainable Development: Challenges and Growth

Dr. Pallavi Sinha Das

The twenty-first century has been referred to as the 'urban' or 'metropolitan' century (Clarke: 2009). It is broadly accepted that for the first time, the majority of the world's population lives in what can be loosely classified as 'urban areas'. By 2050, 66% of people are projected to be living in urban areas, with the highest rates of urban growth expected in low and middle-income countries. India, followed by China and Nigeria, will account for 37% of projected growth in urban populations (Satterthwaite: 2007). Rapid Urban growth is supposed to take place because of the existent and perceived benefits of the clustering of human activity, be it economic or social in areas of close proximity (Henderson, 2002). Urban centers offer economies of scale in productive enterprises and public investment. Perceived opportunities such as better and more diverse jobs, improved services and the potential for better infrastructural facilities for improved quality of life attract people to urban areas (Hildebrand: 2013). Urban centers are also social melting pots, centers of innovation which drive towards social change.

However, the pace and degree of urbanization poses significant challenges for the cities which are noticeable in the form of social differentiation, poverty, conflict and environmental degradation.

Unplanned urban expansion which may negatively influence the economic and social well-being of the people living in the area, contributing to congestion of space, poor housing facilities, pressure on limited public services, air and water pollution and associated health issues (Mitlin & Satterthwaite, 2012). Cities occupy 0.5% of the world's land, but they account for an estimated 70% of economic activity, along with 60% of energy consumption, 70% of waste and 70% of greenhouse gas emissions across the globe. The benefits of urban agglomeration are also experienced disproportionately across urban populations. For instance, although access to services is higher in urban areas, for those living at or below the poverty line service quality can be poor and costs extremely high. Certain groups, particularly those in informal settlements, may be marginalized in both access to services and decision-making processes, which further deteriorate the quality of life in the urban area as well as it has a vice-versa effect on the environment of the urban area.

Importance of Sustainability in Urban Development

Urbanization is one of the significant realities of recent decades in India. Its urban system consists of 7,933 cities and towns of different population size, and a population of 377.16 million (Census 2011), the second largest in the world. The urban system has registered an extraordinary expansion over the 2001–11 decade, and this trend is expected to continue. An esti-mated 180 million rural people live to sub-urban area of India's 70 largest ur-ban centres, a number that will increase to about 210 million by 2030 (McKinsey Global Insti-tute, 2010). Better administration of human settlements is of the priority in the less developed and developing countries if the aspirations of citizens, governments and the concerned international community are to be realized. Recognition of this need has been encouraged by a growing awareness that cities, towns, and villages have functions to perform together which is equally important for the rural and urban areas. While urban centers have undergone considerable change, urban systems have been mistreated, resulting almost everywhere a condition which is unacceptable by any guideline. This neglect has not only taken the form of inadequate resources for necessary measures and indifferent approach of institutions capable of performing, but it has also cultivated an uncertainty about the nature of the responsibilities involved for the preservation of the socio-economic development.

Mistakes made in managing urban growth are very hard to overturn. Infrastructure investments, urban land-use systems, and layouts can leave a permanent mark on the environment with the impacts that may be difficult to alter for many decades. Without adequate management and investments, slums may expand, and cities may fail to generate the jobs necessary to improve livelihood. As a result, inequalities, exclusion and violence may increase. Cities might fail to decouple economic development from resource use, and cities may fail to provide economic opportunities to surrounding rural areas and become vulnerable to climate and other environmental changes. Cities all around the world are struggling to accommodate their rising populations and address the multi dimensional challenges of urban development. Thus it's high time for us to stand for the rising concerns of the urban sustainable development for this reason, how cities address the challenge is of paramount importance today. The call for urban sustainable development of the area is an attempt to respond to the past overlook of society, environment and economic standards. Yet much remains confused about the purposes, nature, scope, and distribution of responsibilities which may be meant by the concept of urban sustainable development.

The Guiding principle for urban sustainable development:

Agenda 21 of the Earth Summit addresses the idea of 'sustainable development' of cities. It mandates concrete planning and also implies conceptual guidelines that should guide the planning generally. The 'concrete 'plans proposed in Agenda 21 include equity, entrepreneurship, technology transfer, access to land, security of land tenure, tenants' rights, liberalized credit policies and low-cost building material programs to 'sustainable'' urban living for the homeless and for the urban poor. It asks developing countries to encourage small businesses in the informal economic sector and developed countries to provide developing countries monetary and technical aid. Within nations, wealthy districts are asked to provide clean water, sanitation, and waste collection services to poorer ones. It also proposes a number of substantial strategies like suitable technology, transport reform and urban revitalization. Governments are asked to improve slums and also to build cities invulnerable to natural disasters. National construction programs using local and non-polluting technologies are also encouraged. In terms of planning principle, however, Agenda 21 introduces paradigm of urban development. This paradigm actually relates to bringing sustainability to city planning practice.

Urbanization issues in India:

Social- Economic Indicators of Urban India:

Significant challenge is to regenerate the urban hub which has a typical feature of mushrooming slums, overburdened infrastructure, insufficient open spaces and poor quality of life. Also the effort to conserve the heritage and maintain social and cultural history is missing. Urban India is plagued by shortage of housing facilities and scarcity of land for social overheads like roads, footpaths, parks, schools and so on. The roots of these problems can be found in the inadequate and unfair land policy of the country. No distinctions has been made between revenue expenditure and capital expenditure at the urban local government level, perhaps because of an accounting convention or because their capital expenditure tends to be very small. This is a very serious problem considering the huge urban infrastructure deficit in Indian cities. Two important studies -High Powered Expert Committee (HPEC Ahluwalia 2011) and McKinsey (2010) have brought out how Indian municipalities are under-spending in core infrastructure like transport, water supply, sewerage, drainage, etc. for decades, striking at the very root of the country's potential for economic growth and prosperity. Since total municipal revenue for the country as a whole was estimated at about Rs 1 lakh crore, and bulk of this goes towards staff salaries, pensions, and operational expenses, the urban local governments are in no position to meet the huge capital expenditure requirements.(Magla, khare, Roy, Mathur, Mohantany Aluwalia: 2019) Around 30% of the urban population in India live in poor quality, overcrowded accommodation with inadequate or no provision for basic infrastructure and services (National Institute of Urban Affairs (NIUA) 2011). According to the 2011 Census, the urban population grew to 377.1 million as compared to 286.1 million in 2001 census showing a growth of 2.76 percent per annum during 2001-2011. The level of urbanization in the country as a whole increased from 25.7 percent in 1991 to 27.82 percent in 2001 and to 31.14 percent in 2011 – an increase of 3.3 percentage points during 2001-2011 compared to an increase of 2.1 percentage points during 1991-2001.They are also the ones who can least afford high transportation costs, live on the periphery and hence system contributes to a self-perpetuating cycle of poverty. They also face legal barriers to get access to electricity, land tenancy, power connections with an impact on safety of the end users. It deepens the cultural, economic and social gap between rich and poor and hence poses real hindrance to attaining sustainability. (Ministry of Housing and Urban Poverty Alleviation, GOI: 2014)

In 2001, about 23.5 per cent of the urban households were living in slums, which signifi-cantly reduced to 17 per cent in 2011. Howev-er, the absolute number of households living in slums has increased from 10.15 million in 2001 to 13.75 million in 2011. The mega cities of Greater Mumbai, Delhi NCR and Kolkata house about 42 to 55 per cent of their popula-tion in slums, whereas the proportion of slum dwellers and urban poor in the millionplus cities is around 35 per cent. Access to basic amenities like drinking water, electricity, septic tank or flush and toilet facilities are the major determinants of quality of urbanization. Estimates at the state and national level collected from National Sample Survey for all the four components have shown an improvement over the year 2001 to 2011. For example, the uses of septic-tank / flush by households in urban areas have increased from 70.7 percent in 2002 to 81.6 percent in 2012. In the year 2012, 97.9 percent households in urban India had access to electricity, which shows an improvement of over 6 percentage points over 91.6 percent estimated in 2002. Nagaland, Dadra & Nagar Haveli, Daman &

Diu, Goa, Lakshadweep, Mizoram and Sikkim topped on this aspect with all the households having access to electricity in 2012. Bihar was at the bottom of this list with only 89.20 percent urban households having access to electricity in 2012.

Literacy level and educational attainment are vital indicators of development in a society. According to census 2011, Urban India was 84.1 percent literate. Uttar Pradesh and Jammu & Kashmir had the lowest urban literacy at 75.10 percent and 77.10 percent respectively, in the year 2011. The urban sex ratio and child sex ratio at national level has increased from 894 in 1991 to 929 (female per thousand male) in 2011. States like Gujarat, Daman & Diu and Dadra & Nagar Haveli saw a huge decline in urban sex ratio from 1991 to 2011. On the other hand, the child sex ratio at country level declined from 906 in 2001 to 905 in 2011.

Employment generation is one of the main challenges for policy makers in India so as to utilize the demographic dividend and boost economic growth. It is important to create adequate jobs in urban areas so that migratory labor force can be employed in more productive sectors such as manufacturing and services. Workforce participation rate in urban India was 35.5% in 2011-12 up from 33.7% in 1999-2000. The known fact is providing decent work in the organized sector, is greatest challenges in India

Water Supply, Sewerage and Solid Waste

There is a tremendous pressure on civic infrastructure systems like water supply, sewerage and drainage, solid waste management, etc. The availability of water supply ranges from four hours or less per day in Delhi, Ban-galore and Hyderabad to nine hours in Kolkata. A household study conducted in seven cities in India found that the average per capita consump-tion of water is 92 litres per capita per day (lpcd), which is close to the WHO guideline of 100 lpcd for optimal access. Further analysis of the data by socio-economic quintiles shows that water con-sumption increases with a rise in socio-economic status, although the inter-quintile differences are not significant.(GOI report: Habitat III 2016) As per 2011 census only 32.7 percent households have piped sewerage connections and 37 percent of total waste water is treated in urban India. Solid waste systems are severally stressed. The state of services reflects the deterioration in the quality of city environments. India produces 62 million tones of urban waste annually, out of which 5.6m tonnes consist of plastic waste, 0.17m constitute of biomedical waste, 7.90m tonnes constitute hazardous waste while 15 lakh ton is e-waste. The total waste generation is estimated 165 million tonnes by 2030. (Central Pollution Control Board : Report 2019)

Studies reveal that India discards around 0.6 m tonnes of plastic waste into oceans annually. It has been ranked as 12th in producing plastic waste and has been ranked as 10 th for generation of municipal solid waste. It is 5th in generating e-waste. Only 43 million tonnes (MT) of the waste is collected, 11.9 MT is treated and 31 MT is dumped in landfill sites. Experts believe that India is following a flawed system of waste disposal and management they have also expressed concern on the process as more than three-fourth of solid waste management budget is allotted to collection and transportation, leaving very little for processing and disposal.

Urban Transport

Most of the cities in India have been facing urban transport problems for last many years, which have negatively affected the mobility of people and trade and industry growth of the urban areas. These problems are due to prevailing imbalance in the transportation system; inadequate transport infrastructure and its sub-optimal use; no integration between land use and transportation planning; and little development in city bus services, which promote the disinterest of people in public transport. In view of this, the Government of India approved the National Urban Transport Policy (NUTP) in April 2006. The challenge for improved bus transport is to provide good quality service at affordable prices. It is important to evaluate alternative public transport technologies in the context of city characteristics. However the size and population of a city is very important for selecting the suitable mode of transport as well as implementing public transport system. Apart from all these road congestion, acute shortage of parking spaces both on and off the streets, the severity of air pollution needs an immediate attention, of 180 Indian cities; there is a wide variation in the pollution concentration and severity across cities. (Kamyotra et al., 2012) Air pollution in Indian cities is the fifth leading cause of death in India. Annually, about 620,000 premature deaths occur due to air pollution in Indian cities (Roy, chowdhury, 2013). Premature deaths due to air pollution occur as a consequence of cardio-vascular ailments. Over a decade, air quality management attempts have met with mixed responses. Toxic air and its effects on health are seriously compromising the 'livability' of Indian cities. The anther major concern is of road safety in most of the Indian cities, non-motorized modes like cycling and walking presently share the same right of way as cars and two-wheelers leading to unsafe conditions for all (National Urban Transport Policy (NUTP), 2015). The number of fatalities is also increasing in relation to the increasing motorization and higher slow-moving vehicles in the traffic stream. While progress has been made towards protecting people in cars, the needs of vulnerable groups of road users, primarily cyclists and pedestrians, are not being met. Each city has its own unique history, characteristics and related problems, but problems in urban cities in India are characteristically similar to other cities in developing countries.

Urban Ecosystem and Biodiversity

By urban biodiversity we mean the variety and richness of living organisms and habitat diversity found in and on the edge of human settlements.(Muller et al., 2010) Urban biodiversity is concerned primarily with environmental improvement, control of air and noise contamination and microclimatic variation. Accelerated urban growth presents several intricate challenges for the natural environment in Indian cities and increasing water pollution and air pollution has become a integral part of ecosystem. A continuous infringement and alteration of ecosystems from woodlands, grass lands, coastal areas, wetlands and water bodies into urban concrete jungles further degrading them (Nagendra : 2012). The remaining green spaces in many cities have been transformed from their original state and species spaces to human-designed, landscaped and pesticide-intensive parks.

The soaring population density in many cities and towns creates particular challenge to minimize the impact of climate change. A major challenge will be to manage scarcities and excesses of water. Coastal and inland cities located near rivers, such as Mumbai, Kolkata, and Delhi has to deal with increased risk and intensity of flooding every year. The most vulnerable urban residents tend to be socio-economically deprived people as they tend to live in informal or traditional settlements, located in areas at greatest risk of flooding or landslides and the risk of deportation is high during environmental crises. Another major element of change because of urbanization takes place along the coastlines through the growth of existing coastal cities and projected and ongoing expansion of new ports. This threatens important coastal regions and leads to destruction of habitats such as mangroves and sea turtle nesting beaches, and increased demand for fish, turtle eggs and other seafood. Building construction close to the shoreline, along with mangrove destruction, also leaves cities more vulnerable to flooding and other damage from natural disasters like cyclones and tsunamis, and projected sea level rise from global climate change. Future development along the coastline must incorporate strategies to maintain and restore natural vegetation as a buffer along the water's edge. (Puthucherril 2011) Poverty and inequity in cities presents an especial challenge for environmental governance.

In India, more than 58.6 per cent of the landmass is prone to earthquakes of moderate to very high intensity; over 12 per cent of its land is prone to floods and river erosion; close to 5,700 km out of the 7,516 km long coastline is prone to cyclones and tsunamis; 68 per cent of its cultivable area is vulnerable to droughts; and, its hilly areas are at risk of landslides and avalanches. During the last 15 years, the country has experienced major earthquakes, cyclones and floods. In view of the higher urban population density and growing ur-banization, this disaster profile of the country has special significance for urban areas with a need for planned approach for disaster risk reduction. United Nations Global Assessment Report (GAR, 2015) on disaster risk estimates the country's av-erage annual economic loss due to disasters to be U.S. $9.8 billion, of which U.S. $7 billion loss is on account of floods.(Kundu and Thakur: 2006)

In recent times Indian cities have witnessed re-peated incidences of urban flood. Urbanization leads to developed catchments, which increases the flood peaks from 1.8 to 8 times and flood vol-umes by six times. Consequently, flooding occurs very quickly, sometimes within few minutes, re-sulting in cities being inundated over a few hours to several days. The impact can also be wide-spread, including temporary relocation of people, damage to civic amenities, deterioration of water quality and risk of epidemics.

Urban Governance

Indian cities do not hold empowerment within the Indian federal structural to take up the challenges of urbanization with rapid growth. The Constitution of India has originally placed the accountability for urban development on state governments. In 1992, the 74th Constitutional Amendment officially documented urban local bodies as the third tier of government and made laws related to that state governments transfer various powers to local governments a set of specified functions under the 12th Schedule, handing over to them the responsibility for functions such as urban planning, including town planning; regulation of land use and construction of buildings, roads, and bridges; the provision of water; public health; and sanitation and solid waste management. As a result, accountability now rests with the urban local bodies but their lies the gap in the planning, the urban local bodies not only lack finances but also the capacity for planning and management. They had been given the responsibility for the development of the area but they do not have sufficient authority in their hands.

Town planning plays a significant role because it is an powerful instrument for mobilizing finances in a transparent manner to help meet the growing investment needs for urban infrastructure. Municipal functionaries in most cases are employees of the state governments and are posted by the state government to individual cities and therefore they lack the attention in ever growing problems of the city areas.

On funding, the 74th Constitutional Amendment had required that state finance commissions be set up by the state governments to spell out the principles for transference of the revenue part from the state government to local governments (Mathur & Peterson: 2006). The expectation was that states will follow the standard set by the Government of India in appointing highly reputed members and chairpersons to the Central Finance Commission, providing technical support to the commission, and accepting its recommendations n the various developmental activities (Rangarajan: 2005). However, state finance commissions did not meet the standards set by the Central Finance Commission. They have not challenged the state level political resistance to devolve and urban local governments have remained cramped by the lack of funds and are functioning with unfunded mandates.

The latest available data show deterioration in almost all of the major financial indicators of empowerment for urban local governments in India from their already very low levels. While cities are expected to act as engines of growth in the coming decades, municipal finances in India remain underdeveloped. Municipal revenue continues to account for a small share of GDP in India, and has remained stagnant at around 1 per cent of GDP during the period from 2007-08 to 2017-18. (Magla, khare, Roy, Mathur, Mohantany Aluwalia: 2019) The constitution also requires to make changes in the working of metropolitan planning committees (MPCs) and district planning committees (DPCs) they should prepare development plans for their respective areas, although there is lack of clarity on how these plans will fit into a larger picture and how they will be financed and therefore it can be said that Indian urbanization is by default not by design.

Way Forward for Sustainable Cities

As cities are ever-changing, composite and inter-connected system, therefore intervention in one facet of urbanization will influence the other. Subsidiary benefits of a particular policy goal can help drive the implementation of the policy and sustain it in long term, but only when the inherent risk can be managed. For e.g climate change will worsen the pressure on city infrastructure Ministry of Urban Development. The Government of India has launched Nation Mission for Sustainable Habitat (NMSH) to address urbanization challenges (Planning Commission 2013c; National Institute of Urban Affairs (NIUA) 2011). Government of India has also launched Smart Cities Mission (SCM) on 25 June 2015 for 5-year period with the objective of promoting smart cities that provide core infrastructure and give a decent quality of life to its citizens, a clean and sustainable environment and application of Smart' Solutions. The strategic components of Smart City initiative are area-based development involving city improvement (retrofitting), city renewal (redevelopment) and city extension (Greenfield development) plus a Pan-city development in which Smart Solutions are applied covering larger parts of the city. Based on an AllIndia Competition, 100 smart cities, as targeted, have been selected in various Rounds ensuring that at least one city will be selected from each state/UT. (MoUD: 2010)

Apart from these Indian government has adopted various measures to bring in sustainable urban growth in the country, they are as follows:

Pradhan Mantri Awas Yojana (PMAY) or the "Housing for All by 2022" scheme addresses the housing requirements of the urban poor, including slum dwellers, and provides provision of houses for all urban poor over a period of seven years. The policy focuses on eradication of the gap between supply and demand, and improving the living condition of the urban poor including slum population; Rise in self-ownership of all-weather, sustainable and disaster resilient dwelling units

Rental Housing: Ministry of Housing and Urban Affairs has drafted a National Urban Rental Housing Policy, 2016, which would encourage promotion of rental housing for various segments of people and create adequate rental housing stock by promoting Social Rental Housing (SRH). The special focus is on affordability of houses of vulnerable groups and urban poor through promoting shelter facilities and also development of need based rental housing for specific target groups.

Housing for Migrant Population: Ministry of Housing and Urban Affairs has set up a working group to study the impact of migration on housing, infrastructure and livelihood in urban areas so that appropriate supply market catering to migrant population of various income segments can be devised along with infrastructure and livelihood support programmes.

Also in 2009, Rajiv Awas Yojana (RAY) was launched in pursuance of the vision for "slum free India" where in financial support was extended for providing housing, improvement of basic civic infrastructure and social amenities, creating rental housing stock and transit housing.

(Ministry of Housing and Urban Poverty Alleviation, GOI : 2016).

Swachh Bharat Mission (SBM): In 2014, the Government of India launched the Swachh Bharat Mission : Clean India Mission, which is being implemented by Ministry of Urban Development (MoUD) and by Ministry of Drink-ing Water and Sanitation (MoDWS) for urban and rural areas, respectively. The objectives of the Mission include the following:

- Elimination of open defecation
- Eradication of manual scavenging
- Modern and scientific municipal solid waste management
- To effect behavioural change regarding sanitation practices
- Generate awareness about sanitation and its linkage with public health

- To create an enabling environment for private sector participation in Capex (capital expenditure) and Opex (operation and maintenance expenditure)

The Mission strategy involves Comprehensive Sanitation Planning which includes (i) City Sanitation Plans, (ii) State Sanitation Con-cept, and (iii) State Sanitation Strategy. This will enable an environment for private sector par-ticipation, capacity building and special-focus groups. In the next three years, over 10 million toilets are proposed to be constructed under the Mission. (MoUD, GOI :2014).

Considerable progress has been made over the past few decades to provide access to safe drink-ing water in urban and rural areas. India's population with access to an improved drinking water source has increased, as a result of several programmes initiated at the city level, the access to improved sources of water has in-creased from 88 per cent in 1990 to 97 per cent in 2010 in urban areas. There are some good practices developed for the provision of 24X7 water supplies in major cities in India based on partnership approach. The proportion of total population of India with access to improved sanitation has nearly doubled in the last 20 years, from 18 per cent in 1990 to 34 per cent in 2010. In urban areas, the same has increased from 51 per cent in 1990 to 58 per cent in 2010, and the proportion of population with no sanitation facil-ities has declined from 28 per cent to 14 per cent during the same period.

The proportion of total population of India with access to improved sanitation has nearly doubled in the last 20 years, from 18 per cent in 1990 to 34 per cent in 2010. In urban areas, the same has increased from 51 per cent in 1990 to 58 per cent in 2010, and the proportion of population with no sanitation facil-ities has declined from 28 per cent to 14 per cent during the same period. A considerable portion of urban poor are de-pendent on community/public toilets. Many of these toilets have inadequate water supply and are not connected to the city sewerage system. Efforts are however being made to address this issue. A silver lining has emerged in recent years with a few successful cases of better service provision in water supply and sewerage network cover-ing the core urban areas and building of sewage treatment plants. Alandur Sewerage Project of Maharashtra is one such successful example. (Handbook of Urban Statistics: 2019))

The Union Ministry of Environment, Forests and Climate Change (MoEF&CC) has notified the Solid Waste Management Rules, 2016. This document gives a step-by-step guide (segregation, transporta-tion, treatment and disposal) for waste management. Besides municipal bodies, Non-Governmental Organizations (NGOs), Community Based Or-ganizations (CBOs) and private companies are usually involved in the collection of solid waste. With a view to implement modern and scientific municipal solid waste management practices in Indian cities, the Swachh Bharat Mission targets to achieve 100 per cent collection, transporta-tion, processing and disposal of solid wastes in all statutory towns in a phased manner.

Addressing Climate Change and Creating a Sustainable Habitat

India adheres to the provisions of the two inter-national treaties of 2015. One, the adoption of the Sustainable Development Goals (SDG) in September 2015, which replaced the Millennium Development Goals, set the development agenda for the next 15 years, and two, the Climate Change Agreement under the United Nations Framework Convention on Climate Change (UNFCCC) in Paris in December 2015 which aims at keeping the rise in global temperatures below 2°C, to set the world towards a low carbon, resilient and sus-tainable future.

(U.N. Global Assessment Report:2015

32 Indian States and Union Territories have put in place the State Action Plan on Climate Change (SAPCC) attempting to mainstream cli-mate change concerns in their planning process. As a step towards implementing urban climate related actions, to enhance the knowledge about climate change impacts, Indian Network for Cli-mate Change Assessment (INCCA) was launched in October 2009.

Initiatives for reducing air pollution Green Highways (Plantation and Main-tenance) Policy was launched to develop 140,000 km. long "treeline" along the sides of national highways. (Central Pollution Control Board of India: Report: 2019)

- Green India Mission (GIM) aims to in-crease the forest/ tree cover up to 5 mil-lion hectares (mha) and improve the quality of forest/tree cover on another 5 mha of forest/ non-forest lands combin-ing livelihood support.
- India aims to improve fuel standards by switching from Euro 4 to Euro 6 across the country. First passenger vehicle fuel-efficiency standards have been finalized.
- The Fly Ash Utilization Policy makes it mandatory to use only fly ash/ fly ash-based products in construction of buildings, roads and reclamation/ compaction of land within a radius of 100 km from a coal-based thermal power plant, thus displacing the use of cement. It also man-dates utilization of fly ash for backfilling or stowing of the mines.
- Currently, 586 ambient air quality mon-itoring stations are operational, covering 246 cities, towns and industrial areas. Government of India has released a new four coloured classification scheme for industries, based on their pollution levels.
- India Green House Gas (GHG) Programme is a voluntary programme to support development of India-specific emission factors and for corporates to measure their carbon footprints.
- For promotion of alternative fuels under National Bio-Fuel Policy of 2009, blend-ing of 20 per cent bio-ethanol in gasoline and 20 per cent bio-diesel in diesel by the year 2017 has been targeted. Five per cent blending of ethanol with gasoline has been taken up by the Oil Marketing Companies (OMCs) in 20 states and four Union Territories.

- Auto LPG Dispensing Stations (ALDS) have been established in 232 cities/towns.

Disaster risk reduction initiatives On 1st June 2016, Prime Minister of India has released a National Disaster Management Plan (NDMP) for a comprehensive and dynamic strategy to deal with any kind of disaster. This policy framework is also in conformity with the Interna-tional Strategy for Disaster Reduction, the Rio Declaration, the Millennium De-velopment Goals, the Hyogo Framework (2005–15), the Sendai Framework for Di-saster Risk Reduction (2015–30), and the Sustainable Development Goals (September 2015) and COP 21 (December 2015) with the objective of promoting community-based disaster management, capacity development, consolidation of past ini-tiatives, cooperation with agencies at the national, regional and international levels and coordination to generate a multi-sectoral synergy.

India has developed its own building-energy-rating system named GRIHA which is based on 34 criteria such as site planning, conservation and efficient utilization of resources, to name a few. A number of buildings, including Commonwealth Games Village, have been rated using GRIHA system. Indira Paryavaran Bhawan, i.e., the headquarters of Central Government's Ministry of En-vironment, Forest and Climate Change is a model building of Government of India and has re-ceived LEED India Platinum and a 5-Star GRIHA rating. It is a "Net Zero Energy" building with 100 per cent onsite power generation. India has demarcated vulnerable areas on the coasts and declared them as Coastal Regulation Zone (CRZ) with restrictions imposed on setting up of industries, operations and processes in these areas. India is also implementing programmes for Integrated Coastal Zone Manage-ment (ICZM). The vision of the project is to build national capacity for imple-mentation of comprehensive coastal management. Mapping and demarcation of coastal hazard lines for development of emergency response plans is being carried out in all the coastal states and union territories. Another initiative to protect coastal livelihood is "Mangroves for the Future (MFF)", coordinated by Internation-al Union for Conservation of Nature (IUCN) in India. The government notified the Island Protection Zone (IPZ) in 2011 which focuses on disaster-risk reduction through bio-shields with local vegetation (mangroves) and other soft protection measures, and the conserva-tion of beaches and sand dunes. (Ministry of New and Renewable energy Report: GOI)

For improving urban governance in India apart from the delegation of power in the form of 73rd and 74th amendment government has laid the foundation in the form of community participation Law, disclosure of lands, shift from a cash based accounting to ac-crual-based accounting system, right to public services, Ombudsman Act etc.

Transparency and accountability have assumed primacy in the context of the emerging patterns of relationships between the government and other stakeholders who have begun to play a larger role in managing and financing cities. The JnNURM envisages the enactment of a Public Disclosure Law (PDL) to ensure release of quarterly performance information to all stakeholders. It requires that municipalities and para-statal agencies will have to publish information about the munici-pality and its functioning on a periodic basis. Community participation is vital especially for the programmes meant to address the social causes, which require sup-port from the community for its success. (Teri: Report 2010)

In the recent years, many cities use tools like Geographical Information System (GIS) to improve urban land management and make it more transparent. M-governance application has resulted in high participation as users for internet are far less than that of mobile technology. Therefore, combining mobile technology with Information and Communication Technology (ICT) made it easier to reach out to a large number of people. (Pandey: 2012)

The issues can be numerous and varied for attaining sustainable urban development, But all of them should consider economic, social and environmental aspects of development. In the end it can be said that economic growth does not mean economic development. True economic development should contribute to increase in efficiency and quality of life of a community (Opp, 2008). Rapid urbanization is phenomenon in India but the challenges like vast population; shortage of resources; scale and state of planning; stakeholder's non-participation, etc. has put up pressure on the government. The enormity of the problems needs solution which should be people centric and realistic. All stakeholders including citizen, policy-maker, designer, planner, activist, administrator, politician, etc. should participate and share their responsibilities towards safeguarding our future. They should understand the constraints that prevent success and take a value based action.

To cope up with the challenges, to improve the quality of urban life, it's essential to prioritize the sustainability issue. India has evolved strong framework of policies and programs, legal provisioning, structured institutional arrangement, technological advancement and sustainable measures for development. But this seems to be only a stepping stone and there is a need to develop research, generate inclusive and cohesive database, to bring more transparency and technological inputs and put effort for good governance.

References

Corfee-Morlot, J., Kamal-Chaoui, L., Donovan, M.,Cochran, I., Robert, A. & Teasdale, P. (2009). *Cities,climate change and multilevel governance*. Paris:OECD.

Satterthwaite, D. (2007). *Climate change andurbanization: Effects and implications for urbangovernance*. New York: UNDESA.

Henderson, V. (2002). Urbanization in developing countries. *World Bank Research Observer*

Hildebrand, M., Kanaley, T. & Roberts, B. (2013).*Sustainable and inclusive urbanization in Asia Pacific*.(Strategy Paper). New York: UNDP.

Amin, A. et al., 2013. Planning and design for sustainable urban mobility - Global Report on Human Settlements 2013, UN Habitat.

Mitlin, D. & Satterthwaite, D. (2012). *Urban poverty in the global south: Scale and nature*. Abingdon: Routledge.

Bose, *Studies in India's Urbanization, 1901-1971* (Bombay: Tata McGraw Hill,1973).*https://www.worldbank.org/en/topic/urbandevelopment/brief/solid-waste-management*

C Rangarajan, Dev, S.M. & K. Sundaram, 2014. Report of the Expert Group to review the methodology for measurement of poverty, Available at: http://planningcommission.nic.in/reports/genrep/pov_rep0707.pdf.

Mohan, R., 2014a. India Transport Report - Moving India to 2032 (Volume I - Executive Summary),

Roychowdhury, A., 2013. Good News & Bad News: Clearing the Air in Indian Cities, Centre for Science and Environment.

WHO, 2013. Global status report on road safety 2013 - Supporting a decade of action. Available at: http://www.who.int/iris/bitstream/10665/78256/1/9789241564564_eng.pdf [Accessed AUG 1, 2020].

Aggarwal, S., & Butsch, C. (2012). Environmental and ecological threats in Indian mega-cities. In M. Richter & U. Weiland (Eds.), *Applied urban ecology: A global framework*. Chichester: Blackwell Publishing Ltd.

Nagendra, H., & Gopal, D. (2011). Tree diversity, distribution, history and change in urban parks. *Urban Ecosystems, 14*, 211–223.

United Nations Human Settlements Programme (UN-HABITAT). State of Asian Cities 2010/11 report, United Nations Human Settlements Programme (UN-HABITAT) and the United Nations Economic and Social Commission for Asia and the Pacific (ESCAP). Fukuoka: UN-HABITAT and ESCAP.

Kundu A. and S. Thakur (2006). Access to drinking water in urban India: An Analysis of emerging spatial pattern in the context of new system of governance In *Managing Water Resources: Policies, Institutions and Technologies*, V. Ratna Reddy and S. Mahendra Dev eds. Oxford, New Delhi.

Puthucherril, T. G. «Operationalising integrated coastal zone management and adapting to sea level rise through coastal law: where does India stand?» The International Journal of Marine and Coastal Law 26 (2011) *https://fincomindia.nic.in/writereaddata/html_en_files/fincom15/StudyReports/State% 20of%20 Municipal%2 0Finances% 20in% 20India.pdf accessed on 27july, 5:10p.m*

Ministry of Housing and Urban Poverty Alleviation, Government of India (2016). State Housing Policy for Urban Areas 2016

·Ministry of Urban Development, Government of India (2014). Guidelines for Swachh Bharat Mission

United Nations Office for Disaster Risk Reduction (2015). Global Assessment Report on Disaster Risk Reduction: Making Development Sustainable, the Future of Disaster Risk Management.

Government of India, Central Pollution Control Board of India: Report: 2019

Ministry of Housing and Urban Poverty Alleviation, Government of India (2014). Inclusive Urban Planning: State of the Urban Poor Report 2013. Oxford University Press

Ministry of New and Renewable Energy, Government of India. http://www.mnre.gov.in/

Tata Energy Research Institute (2010). Enhancing Public Participation through Effective Functioning of Area Sabhas. TERI and Energy Research Institute, Ministry of Urban Development, Government of India. http://www.teriin.org/themes/sustainable/pdf/Area_Sabhas.pdf

Pandey, K.K. (2012). Theme Paper for the 56th Members' Annual Conference: Administration of Urban Development and Urban Service Delivery. Indian Institute of Public Administration, New Delhi. http:// www.iipa.org.in/upload/Theme%20Paper%20 Members% 20Conference. pdf

Opp. Susan M. (2008). Roles and realities. In *Local Sustainable Urban Development in a Globalised World,* Lauren C. Heberle and Susan M. Opp eds. Hampshire, Ashgate Publishing Limited, England.

Chapter 5

Search of Space in John Osborne's Look Back in Anger

Rwiti Biswas

Introduction

The word "space" has wide-ranging implications. But the meaning of the word only varies when we look into the same word with varied perspectives. In this paper, an attempt has been made to draw attention of the readers to the physical and emotional angles associated with the word, space and then finding its scope with respect to the city conditions in today's post-modern world as well as with the structure which was prevalent amidst the strict principles with an added tint of disillusionment functioning, in the Victorian British cityscape of the 1950s, that is the most evident in John Osborne's highbrow spectacle, Look Back in Anger. According to the article, "Space - Physics and Metaphysics"; Encyclopedia Britannica (Archived from the original on 6th May, 2008), physical "space is the boundless three-dimensional extent in which objects and events have relative position and direction". Consistent with the psychological understanding of the term, space is defined as "lived in" space of a person or an object which can be further subdivided into three differing categories namely, oriented space, feeling space, and open space. Oriented space is something that deals in the body, in respect to physical objects and its positions, feeling space is the way in which our "psychological and emotional atmosphere is created and felt", whereas, open space is associated to "formless dimension". In that case, we can infer that physical space runs parallel in meaning to oriented space, leaving aside feeling space, which is unique in its kind and intangible in form.

But how can space be defined in an easier expression? Normally, when we look around ourselves, we can feel our bodies been enveloped in a packet of space, a space that might be physically visible or sometimes physically invisible, but never absent. Looking at our surroundings, we find tall buildings and crowded areas everywhere (that is, oriented space), as a part of the urban landscape that can also be regarded as city spaces or cityscapes. Uniformly, according to the Oxford English Dictionary, a cityscape is "the visual appearance of a city or urban area; i.e., a city landscape".

Considering some of the fragments from our school curriculum under subjects like Environmental Education, Geography or sometimes Science as a whole, we recollect reading about a specific section of people 'migrating' to the cities from villages or towns in order to earn a better livelihood. People change their places and shift to a completely new location as it is believed that cities have access to better money earning engagements, job opportunities and infrastructure to support living in a more superior manner. Going by this pattern, cities have now become over populated. Cityscapes are left with no more open spaces. Every open space is day by day undergoing construction to meet the immense requirement of prospective residences as people are increasing in number within a confined boundary (be it the boundary of the domestic walls that make a house, or the state boundaries or the national boundaries, that separate nations and cultural identities). Everywhere we are surrounded by structures, multi storey buildings with multiple souls being caged inside. The minimum physical space which is required to maintain a healthy balance with oneself is lost. People, who belong to the middle or the upper classes, can afford to maintain a polished lifestyle that engages oneself in dwelling in these multi storey structures. And the remaining ones, who are the people belonging to the economically weaker group have chosen to live inside the over-crowded, tiny, slum-like houses located in the unfashionable and unpopular spots within the cityscapes. But whatever the status symbol of a family or an individual is, with the gradual increase in population, affordability of physical space to breathe in, is also decreasing. But the spaces in the slums as well as in the multi storeys are alike, where both are reduced to matchbox-like concentration. Job opportunities have shrunk and will assumable shrink even more in the years

Space crunch in the cityscapes has never been a new sight for the city dwellers in the past years as well. Cities have always been a hub for jobs. The saturation point at which job opportunities today might have reached in the cities, has failed to create room for a lot of young people getting employed anymore. And this has been the case since a very long stretch of time. We can therefore find a lot of people residing in cities because their forefathers chose to move in the cities for a better living. But as we find many, dwelling in the cities, we also find the majority of them as not able to afford a better lifestyle just because of financial crisis. This financial crisis emerges in the basic level from the lack of employment opportunities. Families lacking money, send their children to work because of which they fail to receive proper education. As they do not meet the educational standards which might help them to fetch jobs for themselves, these children are again trapped in this endless cycle of poverty. Girl children are married off whereas the boys search for some temporary source of employment to at least support a living. Adding to this, we can notice that finding a house and supporting rent of the same in cities, as well as the cost of other necessities such as food, medicines, clothes and sometimes some other essential, has itself become a huge challenge for the families. Most of the family members are not employed and each family has a lot of children which ultimately add to the unproductive population of the cities even more. Thus there is always a dearth of jobs in comparison to the overwhelming population residing within the cityscapes. Quoting Nobel Laureate and Professor of Economics, Amartya Sen, in his book, Identity and Violence: The Illusion of Destiny, we perceive the present impoverished condition of the globe in a better way.

An astounding number of children are ill fed, ill clad, ill treated, and also illiterate and needlessly ill. Millions perish every week from diseases that could be completely eliminated, or at least prevented from killing with abandon. Depending on where they are born, children can have the means and facilities for great prosperity or face the likelihood of desperately deprived lives. Massive inequalities in the opportunities different people have encourages skepticism about the ability of globalization to serve the interests of the underdogs. Indeed, a hardened sense of frustration is well reflected in the slogans of protest movements of so-called antiglobalization activists.

It might be an imprecise interpretation if we only consider that poverty and unemployment is always followed by lack of education. In this era of booming population, even an enormous portion of the edified mass has failed to secure proper jobs for themselves which they deserve according to the educational qualification they hold, only because of the concerning growth in population. Along with that, as the world is advancing into a more computerized structure, a lot of people are failing to cope up with the demands of a more technical understanding of subjects and skills, which is compelling them to withdraw themselves from a particular set of jobs. Another section of the society buy opportunities to get in a private educational institution and thereafter end up buying jobs with money, because they are able to afford the cost. Similar worldly situation has been narrated by the English playwright, screenwriter and actor, John Osborne in his 1956 play, Look Back in Anger. Jimmy Porter, who is the main character of the play, has failed to secure himself a job, besides being a graduate. He has simultaneously failed in securing a proper living space, which he should have shared with his wife, Alison Porter, only, but is now compelled to let another man in, his friend, Cliff Lewis, to share the expenses of the Victorian attic in which they live. This state of joblessness and confinement within the four walls of the attic has made Jimmy angry. But the anecdote could manage to be super successful amongst the popular mass of the 1950s Britain and the succeeding generations thereafter, only because the play did not solely narrate the tale of Jimmy as an individual identity but the account of the general mass of the time with similar situation of unwaged existence, holding a graduate degree in hand. If we analyze carefully, the play also narrates the story of a huge crowd of today, who have or degrees in hand to satisfy their intellectual hunger but have no job to satisfy their stomachs.

This way, the smothering echo of the post Second World War, Britain could be very protuberantly observed in John Osborne's Look

Back in Anger. The play was initially written as a script to be performed at the Royal Court Theatre, Sloane Square, London, which was premiered on 8th May, 1956 by the English Stage Company. The show was directed by Tony Richardson. Visual arts has always been a medium through which playwrights have communicated to the general mob of the society about the contemporary social, political and economic happenings and crises observed. John Osborne's Look Back in Anger, was set in the cityscape of 1950s Britain but still managed to twin with the landscape of the upcoming modern world since it narrates the story that every cohort at every corner of the world, after its deliverance would relate to. Being situated in the occidental cityscapes of the 1950s, the play can magically mirror the modern cityscapes of the oriental part of the world as well. It can be somehow related to the concept known as historic recurrence, if we consider the characters of the play and their take on everything as real happenings. The idea of historic recurrence can be hinged to many instances in history throughout the world, where similar instances in both conditions have been observed in two entirely dissimilar situations (where the present youth can relate to the hopelessness that Jimmy and Alison had been facing, being a part of the post Second World War Britain). Look Back in Anger's surprising identification with the post modern world can be established as one of its kind.

I. 'Search' of Physical Space

The picture that Osborne had painted of 1950s Britain, was at the time still suffering with the patrimony of the Second World War. Buildings lacked proper nourishment and people were in search of a fitting space to live in. To look for a suitable physical room was a real problem, for the already existing houses could not allot anymore tenants. Look Back in Anger was written strictly in accordance with the unity of place, the idea of which French classicists had derived from Poetics, written by Aristotle in 330 BCE. Unity of place along with the other two unities, that acted as the pivotal point of the plot of the classical plays, namely, unity of action and unity of time, as observed by Aristotle are only based on monitoring how the classical dramas used to function. Thus, the unity of place is a very vexed concept and does not guarantee any proper definition or structure.

Disputes arose over such problems as whether a single day meant 12 or 24 hours and whether a single place meant one room or one city. Some believed that the action represented in the play should occupy no more time than that required for the play's performance-about two hours. In spite of such severe restrictions, the great 17th-century French dramatists, Pierre Corneille and Jean Racine, confining the crises of their characters' lives to a single setting and a brief span of hours, produced a unique form of tragedy that derives its austere power from its singleness of concentration.

John Osborne's Look Back in Anger (1956) similarly, is set in a confined periphery of an attic where three people live, a young married couple, Jimmy and Alison, and a male friend, Cliff. Osborne had very wisely used the theatre-trope of the unity of place, by restricting the actions in the whole play within the four walls of the attic to willfully depict the suffocation that both Jimmy and Alison had been facing, added with the monotony of their daily timetable. This absence of space tells a lot of stories regarding the lacking city spaces in Britain in the post Second World War scenario. But lack of space was not a problem that could solely be associated with war struck Britain and its periphery. What intrigues the readers is that, dearth of city spaces has been a very noteworthy crisis around the globe in this 21st century sphere as well. Experts have observed that this crisis relating to space crunch can take up a larger shape in the coming years of the world.

Images: Photographs of the original production of Look Back in Anger by John Osborne (Royal Court Theatre, 1956) starring Kenneth Haigh as Jimmy Porter, Mary Ure as Alison Porter and Alan Bates as Cliff.

If we carefully observe the initial section of the opening act where stage directions are communicated (instanced below) and the pictures placed above,

The Porters' one-room flat in a large Midland town. Early evening. April. The scene is a fairly large attic room, at the top of a large Victorian house. The ceiling slopes down quite sharply from L. to R. Down R. are two small low windows. In front of these is a dark oak dressing table. Most of the furniture is simple, and rather old. Up R. is a double bed, running the length of most of the back wall, the rest of which is taken up with a shelf of books. Down R. below the bed is a heavy chest of drawers, covered with books, neckties and odds and ends, including a large, tattered toy teddy bear and soft, woolly squirrel. Up L. is a door. Below this a small wardrobe. Most of the wall L. is taken up with a high, oblong window. This looks out on to the landing, but light comes through it from a skylight beyond. Below the wardrobe is a gas stove, and, beside this, a wooden food cupboard, on which is a small, portable radio. Down C. is a sturdy dining table and three chairs, and, below this, L. and R., two deep, shabby leather armchairs. AT RISE OF CURTAIN, JIMMY and CLIFF are seated in the two armchairs R. and L., respectively. All that we can see of either of them is two pairs of legs, sprawled way out beyond the newspapers which hide the rest of them from sight. They are both reading. Beside them, and between them, is a jungle of newspapers and weeklies. When we do eventually see them, we find that JIMMY is a tall, thin young man about twenty-five, wearing a very worn tweed jacket and flannels. Clouds of smoke fill the room from the pipe he is smoking.

We can recognize how congested in a manner, the stage has been willfully set up. When we look at the scene and imagine ourselves to be a part of that structure, we feel smothered. But we also find fiction and non-fiction getting blended when we wake up from this trance like state and realize that the physical conditions in which we are living today in is somewhat a reflection of that small one roomed attic in which Jimmy, Alison and Cliff shared their individual spaces.

II. 'Search' Of Emotional Space

One of the most prominent stumbling blocks in Jimmy and Alison's relationship turned out to be the breakdown in communication that somehow emanated from the lack of secluded latitude for the young couple stemming from the lack of private space for them inside the small one- roomed attic. They had no accessibility to private space that a young couple might readily need to build their relationship stronger, and nourish it. Their privacy in the initial chapter of the play can be found ever interrupted by the presence of Cliff. Cliff inside that one roomed attic had a furniture existence. But neither did Cliff's vegetable existence inside the small room, nor the intrusion of Helena Charles (Alison's friend) in Act II could furthermore negatively affect Jimmy and Alison's relationship to a particular extent because it was already disintegrating without any notable push factor. The problematic aspect in Jimmy and Alison's relationship became more grave and grave-like when they together were not provided with the minimum physical space to sort their emotional distance out, which had originated from the past incidents in both their lives. Alison had become so emotionally distant from her marital life, that she had stopped sharing every major to minute details of her life with her husband, that she even refrained herself from breaking the news of her pregnancy to her husband, because she did not know how he would react to it.

The character of Cliff has been deliberately made by Osborne as a faint attempt to fill in the void existing in between Alison and Jimmy. Cliff has not been romanticized and sexualized throughout the play but somehow he has always acted as a cushion to comfort Alison that Jimmy has never been able to. Cliff has always acted as a medicine to the physical as well as emotional wounds that Jimmy has repeatedly inflicted upon her.

In the play we have, a lot of time come across the act of role playing into a "teddy bear" and a "wooly squirrel" that Jimmy and Alison were engaged in, as an effort to save their dying relationship. This shows how much hollow the relationship between them had become with every passing time. At the end of the play, when things took a better turn and situation normalized between them, we still find them engaging themselves in role playing as an act of love making, that focuses on the fact that they are again surrendering their relationship to the inanimate toys in a faint endeavor to save their relationship for one more time.

Thus, the shortfall of physical space for the young married couple developed into emotional separation. Alison grew more and more physically and emotionally passive towards Jimmy, whereas Jimmy grew more and more aggressive due to the immediate situation he was in. With the population explosion and technological advancements, people are drifting apart from each other as psychologists have observed. In the modern cityscape, with the swell in the number of city dwellers, lack of physical space is observable. Likewise, populaces contained and confined within shrink wrapped houses, similar to Jimmy and Alison are likely to go through the same mechanical failure of individual relationships in the contemporary city spaces.

In cityscapes today, people live an overly fast life with faster communication and stress filled jobs. Taking out time from this restricted schedule, people have found an easier route to diversion that deal in the virtual screens of the neon world and the other sorts of materialistic pleasure. Psychologists today, are of the opinion that emotional distance amongst humans in the current generation is increasing day by day with the noticeable technological furtherance.

Technology has always continued to be a boon for the world, as it has made our lives so easy and comfortable. In this day and age, we have all sorts of mobile applications at our finger tips that enable us to clasp the best of every world. We have innumerable software and computer run programs that can easily quench our intellectual thirst, as well as can satisfy us with whatever we need at our doorstep. But as the world is narrowing down in regard to accessibility to every possible object, the world is witnessing many more splintered relationships because of lack of physical communication. People have cocooned themselves in this alternate reality which has made them drift a thousand metaphorical miles apart from each other.

III. 'Search' of A Befitting Job

Jimmy Porter was angry and his anger had stemmed from a motley array of incidents ranging from his childhood, but the most evident factor triggering his anger was his state of joblessness. By the middle of the decade of the 1950s, the middle class were drowned in the smoky cloud of disillusionment, which had emitted from the chimneys of the good producing factories that would mass-produce consumer goods to meet their buoyant insistence. Technology had come in, and with that, job opportunities had stated to disappear because excess of man power was not needed anymore. Jimmy was a graduate with Oxbridge education. But because of the fact that people were not getting jobs according to their educational qualification, he was compelled to sell sweets at the streets with his friend, Cliff as the sole source of earning. Jimmy was angry with his middle class existence. He was filled in with wrath for not belonging from a privileged class that would fetch him money and a convincing job, just like Nigel (Alison's brother) who was certain to have a steady life ahead, if also he did not possess any individual merit. The sadomasochistic element in Jimmy was encouraged by these factors and the one who suffered the most because of this distorted side of his mental mechanism was, he himself. This was one of the prime reasons why he channelized his anger entirely upon Alison as she by birth was also a representative of the aristocratic class of Britain, and Jimmy thought everyone of them as his combatant. Jimmy in the play is emblematic of the most of the out-of-work youth of the time, who were angry at the government for not securing their future, despite of so many unfounded promises of settling the same, which somehow the current generation belonging to any part of the world can also relate to.

This problem of redundancy associated with the post World War II Britain framework, is highly reflective of the happenings of the upcoming world. Every year in comparison to the number of young graduates in each country, job opportunities are very limited. Few get their desired jobs where the rest go for any other alternative. It's a kind of compromise, people have been doing since years but jobs are always produced in a meager number if compared with the number of eligible candidates appearing every year. Like the population boom and technological advancement in the cityscapes of 1950s Britain had given birth to too many educated workless, Jimmy being no exception, in the coming couple of decades, with the population soar and technological spread, many people will tend to lose their jobs, resulting in people suffering from joblessness and utter disillusionment. The disappointed educated unwaged will thus undesirably rise in number in the nearing years.

The post World War II Britain at the time had experienced a boom in the demand for consumer goods because of the industrialization. The British society had reached a "new era" of "affluence" and "stability" but still, poverty and unemployment could not be eradicated. This materialistic world had seen people suffering from outright disenchantment, which is again a mirrored scenario of today's cityscape where people are symbolically drifting away from each other.

Conclusion

By comparing these completely two different time zones, that is, the 1950s, and the 21st century and years to be followed, one thing we can understand is, neither are Jimmy and Alison fictional characters, nor are these characters time bound. In the modern day city spaces, every other person we look around at, are just like Jimmy and Alison, tired with disaffection. We can find each one of them with a heart full of rupturing relationships and a head full of anger.

Thus, we can conclude that space is missing from every time-frame, that is very essential for comforting an individual in both the physical and emotional terms, be it in the 1950s Britain, or the 2020s modern day world followed by the coming years and because of which relationships are suffering and will continue to suffer for many more years. Currently everywhere we find people starving, the rich getting richer and the poor getting more deprived than always. In addition to the existent critical scenario, situations of war have always created a problem for the middle class mass. The aftermath of the Second World War had left the middle class British youth in a state of crisis where the character of the fictional Jimmy or may be the autobiographical Osborne acted as a spokesperson for thousands of the "angry young men". If we observe globally, nations are fighting against each other or sometimes fighting within themselves, be it for the sake of religious and racial intolerance or over pieces of land, power and authority, and are thus, continually left in a war like state. As we had noted in the case of Jimmy and the bunch of "angry young" crowd having similar complains and demands, the middle class crisis is becoming more and more observant in today's cityscape as the affordability of more and more physical space is dwindling. The prospering population hereafter has to grapple for spaces everywhere, be it managing for a space to live in or arranging for a job opportunity to fit in.

References

Handley, Graham. (1990). John Osborne: Look Back in Anger. Penguin Books.

Osborne, John, and Neeraj Malik. (2002). John Osborne: Look Back in Anger, Worldview.

"Photographs of the Original Production of Look Back in Anger by John Osborne (Royal Court Theatre, 1956)." The British Library, The British Library, 24 Aug. 2017, www.bl.uk/collection-items/photographs-of-the-original-production-of-look-back-in-anger-by-john-osborne-1956.

Sen, Amartya. (2007). Identity and Violence: The Illusion of Destiny. Penguin Books.

The Editors of Encyclopaedia Britannica. (2019) "Unities." Encyclopædia Britannica, Encyclopædia Britannica, Inc., Retrieved from 17 Nov. 2019, www.britannica.com/art/unities.

Welwood, J. (1977). On Psychological Space. Journal of Transpersonal Psychology, 9(2), 97-118. Retrieved from https://psycnet.apa.org/home

Chapter 6

Residential Environment and Well-being among Urban Elderly Apartment Dwellers

Trisha Bakshi

Introduction

History has recorded no society without the existence of old people, but they previously constituted a very small percentage of the total population in any given time or place (Achenbaum, 2005). With the advent of medical science resulting in low fertility, low mortality and improved longevity of human life, the number of elderly (aged at least 60 years) has increased to a considerable extent. The shift in demographics indicating an accelerated growth in the proportion of elderly population across the world demands greater attention to effectuate physical and psychological well-being among the elderly. In India the size and share of people aged 60 years and above is expected to increase from 71 million in 2001 to 173 million by 2026 (Dixit & Goyal, 2015); the rate of growth being greater in comparison to any other population group in the country. This increased life expectancy has wide-ranging socio-economic and political implications in terms of catering to the housing provision, medical care and community-based services to suit the special needs of the elderly (Dapaah & Wong, 2001). According to Harvey (2008) the "quality of urban life has become a commodity, as has the city itself, in a world where consumerism, tourism, cultural, and knowledge based industries have become major aspects of the urban political economy" (Buffel et al., 2019). Alongside population aging causing housing stress, rapid urbanization too necessitates reconfiguration of the city spaces wherein the functional limits of urban sprawl are outstretched by communities to accommodate the ever-increasing number of apartment buildings. Understanding the relation between these two trends has become major issue for public policy making research indispensable on the effects of residential environment on the well-being of the urban elderly. Also, since disintegration of the traditional joint family due to industrialization, westernization and urbanization giving rise to nuclerarisation of family, and thereby, shrinking social support, the elderly often feel isolated if they are not housed properly; the right to adequate housing being one of the basic human rights. Taking into consideration, the changing dynamics of growing old in urban India in the 21st century, this paper calls for a need to focus on the living environment of the elderly, highlighting the factors related to their residential satisfaction to improve the living conditions and hence psycho-physiological well-being and the over-all quality of life during one's twilight years. Since the concept of quality of life is intertwined with that of the quality of the urban environment, adopting an increasingly human-oriented design is the need of the hour (Temeljotov Salaj & Petri?, 2009 as cited in Grum, 2019).

The term elderly has been variously defined by societies it is best to consider the conventional retirement age recognized by a particular society. Hence, those belonging to the age group of 60 years and above are considered as the elderly in India. The International Plan of Ageing adopted by the World Assembly on Ageing in 1982 has also specified the same age category (Dapaah & Wong, 2001). Well-being has been variously defined and often related to positive psycho-social and physical outcomes like (a) quality of family relationships; (b) physical health; (c) decreased disability; d) lower mortality rate; (e) religious involvement; (f) volunteerism; (g) engagement in leisure activities (Erickson & Johnson, 2011). Home is "integral to living" and "an intimate part of older adult's being" (Gillsjo et al., 2011 as cited in Peek et al., 2015), alongside neighborhood as the seniors spend a large portion of their daily time within restricted activity spaces, generally their home or immediate local environments (Oswald, 2005; Kart & Kinney, 2001, as cited in Phillips et al., 2004). This is due to the decreased physical mobility and limited social contact post retirement (Cumming and Henry 1961; Altergott 1988; Oh 2003 as cited in James III, 2008). This makes residential satisfaction, defined as the comparison or evaluation of one's needs and expectations as against the realities of the residential environment (James III, 2008) an important area of investigation when considering well-being among the elderly. However, since residential satisfaction is a multi-faceted and complicated construct and the aged a heterogeneous group, delineating the relationship between living environment and residential satisfaction among the urban elderly apartment dwellers is not a straightforward task.

Literature Review

Population ageing, a wide spread phenomenon in the present society, brings with it a number of challenges. The shrinking size of the family, weak intergenerational bonds due change in conventional value system, decline in care giving opportunities due to fast paced life of the younger generation (Kumar & Khan: 2015) or lack of economic solvency to provide for adequate care-giving (Khan, 2015) and the need to remain confined at home due to physical immobility or cognitive decline (Dixit & Goyal, 2015) that have added to the woes of the elderly, making population ageing and rapid urbanization important issues on the global agenda (Buffel et al., 2017).

The aged often experience higher incidents of frailty among, caused due to reduced strength, bodily imbalance, and exhaustion (Ferrucci et al., 2004 as cited in Heide et al., 2012). Cognitive decline and restricted mobility render the elderly population vulnerable to feelings of social isolation and loneliness. Though a person's genetic factor was important in considering experiences of ageing, his residential environment (e.g. apartment, retirement community, or a single family) influences the state of health in old age (Dey, 2010; Kaulagekar, 2007). Housing dissatisfaction arising out of inability to cope with hazardous living environment like noise, heat, garbage disposal problem, presence of rodents, high crime rates, dilapidated homes, dark streets, inaccessible shopping centers (Byrnes et al., 2006), often lead to chronic mental and physical stress in the urban elderly (James III, 2008). It is, thus, noteworthy mentioning in this context that for urban older adults conceptualizing residential environment should extend beyond the physical structure of home (Foley, 1980) to include the community as a network of resources needed for survival (Stack, 1974), or the neighborhood that is the block where one lives: a geographic, political or economic boundary on the basis of housing conditions, streets or race (Galster, 1997); keeping in mind that it is problematic to provide a social definition of neighborhood that would fit the understanding of all (Byrnes et al., 2006).

Apart from the crucial role of neighborhood in determining good life among the urban elderly, household structure and organization are also important in the lives of the elderly. Since around 65% of the Indian aged population depend on others for their daily maintenance (Tyagi & Paltasingh, 2015), social support received by them from family members, neighbors, relatives and service providers are important. Rajan and Kumar (2003), while stating the importance of support and care in the well-being of the elderly, distinguish between the two terms in that the former indicates financial assistance (pensions and social security), whereas the later is defined as emotional support provided only by family members or by those in co-residence with the older adults. Residential satisfaction depends on fulfillment of one's residential needs in congenial dwelling conditions (Perez et al., 2001; Phillips et al., 2005), feelings of connection with the neighborhood (Dahlberg, 2019), diversity and accessibility to socio-political and civic spaces (Bowering, 2019), formal care received from the community (Kaulagekar, 2007) and on one's household income that gives one greater financial resources to address residential deficiencies through mobility or modification (Schwirian and Schwirian 1993 as cited in Byrnes et al., 2006); greater ability to work beyond officially specified retirement age; have a supportive living environment provided by family members and live in large-complex households with greater number of a surviving children (Rajan & Kumar, 2003) as compared to those residing in simple and nuclear family units (Kertzer, 1995) due to socio-economic vulnerability (Laslett, 1988) to which they might be exposed if their children migrated to other places, whereas in case of those elderly occupying higher socio-economic status the chances of co-residence with children increased (Alter, 1996) substantially (Manfredini & Breschi, 2013). However, in many situations even the "house-rich" or "asset-rich" retirees to grapple with the problem of low to no income hampering their ability to maintain and modify their house to create elderly-friendly living condition (Dapaah & Wong, 2001; Kraus, 1952). But contrary to conventional belief or prevalent stereotype about ageing, aged are not always poor and ill-housed, as most of them are homeowners and have assets higher than that indicated by their income figures alone (Shanas 1969; Pampel & Choldin 1978 as cited in Foley, 1980). Though the degree to which people are able to control their living environment determines their residential satisfaction during young age, such feelings of satisfaction with neighborhood or built environment increased with age (Grum, 2019), more so in case of apartments tenants with access to community services than homeowners burdened with the responsibility of home maintenance, associated frauds, and the economic investment involved (James III, 2008).

Objectives

1. To explore the relationship between living environment and residential satisfaction among the urban elderly apartment dwellers
2. To identity the demographic factors correlated with residential satisfaction
3. To focus on the determinants of residential community and built environment related to housing satisfaction
4. To investigate the social setting/ household structure that guides the residents' choice of their housing in case of apartment owners and tenants

Methods

Participants

Data was collected through in-depth interviews conducted on 70 men and women aged at least 60 years and residing in Kolkata, a metropolitan city in eastern region of India, thereby constituting urban population. The participants were divided in three age groups: 60+, 70+ and 80+. All the elderly professionals have worked in the service sector and reside in home settings. Majority of them are owners of the apartments they are currently residing in while some are tenants. All are married, while 5 of them are widows. All are presently in a sound physical and mental state to take part in the study. Participants were excluded if they had difficulty in communicating due to cognitive impairment.

Procedure

The respondents were chosen by non-probability snow ball sampling technique, based on the researcher's judgment. Due to difficulty in directly recruiting participants who met the research criteria, first one or two people who qualify to participate were chosen from the familiar circle. They were then asked to help locate potential subjects with the required knowledge or traits. More names suggested in turn. Thus, a list of contacts along with their complete addresses is prepared. Each was individually contacted to ask for their availability or willingness to participate in the study.

The research is exploratory in nature where a survey method was followed to collect data through semi-structured questionnaire, dedicating around an hour on an average to interview each respondent. No questionnaire was administered for the face-to-face interviews conducted. The interviews were conducted in a combination of English and Bengali (the latter being the native language is widely spoken by people living in Bengal) and carried out individually even if a spouse was interviewed. Questions revolved around the apartment dwellers type of family organization, intergenerational relations, unit-characteristics that included floor space, their rating of neighborhood and building condition and their overall satisfaction with the residential environment that included both home and community. The study followed mixed method of quantitative and qualitative technique to elicit response through both close and open ended questions in order to allow the respondents answer objectively as well as freely express their opinion pertaining to the theme concerned. Running notes were taken to prevent the loss of information.

Findings and Discussion

For the purpose of this paper, an elderly is defined as one who is at least 60 years since that is the designated retirement age for most of the sectors, barring health and education sector, in the country. The present study uses responses on residential satisfaction from self-declared owners and tenants of apartments choosing thirty-two men and thirty-eight female apartment dwellers from the metropolitan city of Kolkata.

Role of Demographics in Residential Satisfaction

a) Educational qualification Socio-Economic Status: Around seventy four percent of the respondents have completed graduation; fifteen percent of the respondents were post-graduates, with two respondents having doctoral degree. The rest eleven percent have attained lesser educational degrees. Among the respondents, majority of the men were found to be more qualified compared to their female counterparts. Majority of the respondents hail from middle class background (those having an annual income of 3.4-17 lakhs as per National Council of Applied Economic Research-Centre for Macro Consumer Research 2010 annual income data) and have an average household income of around Rs. 33,000 and above per month. Out of seventy respondents, seventy six percent (n=53) belong to middle class while twenty four percent belong to the upper socio-economic classes. Forty-one (out of seventy) respondents are presently employed, with sixty three percent (out of those employed forty-one) having joined work post retirement with the view that they would be able to maintain decent living standards in residential settings of their choice, pay for their own medical exigencies or simply remain engaged "meaningfully". The rest of the respondents, that is, twenty nine out of seventy, are retired, with some dependent on pension, some financially dependent on their child(ren) while the rest draw money from savings accounts or sources like house rent, government and non- government schemes or others. The question centering on household income and housing cost are relevant in indicating the type of apartments the respondents have been able to afford. Most of the respondents (n=48) live in stand-alone apartment while the remaining twenty-two (out of seventy) live in housing communities.

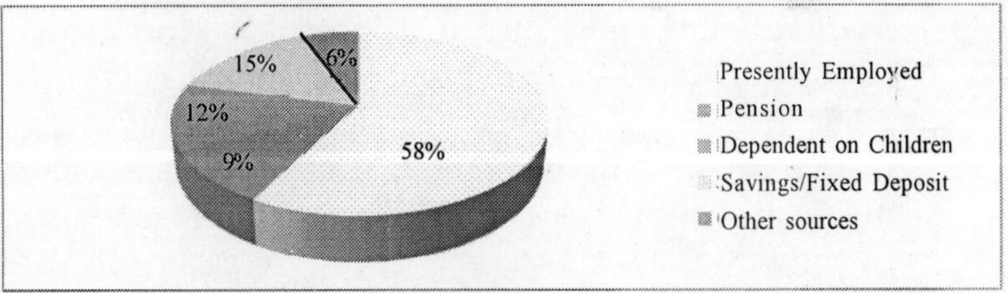

Fig.1. Pie chart showing respondents' present financial status (source of income).

Source: Author's Primary Data

b) Ownership versus Tenantship: Ownership was determined by asking if the respondent or his family member has "bought the apartment", or "rented for cash" or "occupied without cash payment as hereditary property". Out of a total of seventy respondents, only seven percent (n=5) were residing in rented apartment while the remaining sixty five elderly were owners of the apartment they were either currently living in. While ownership was often associated with feelings of greater social status and control over one's residential environment, those residing as tenants neither hinted dissatisfaction from the lack of it nor at limited purchasing power guiding their choice of living arrangement. The temporary nature of their present residence, recent migration to the city or their future plan of relocating to stay with their child (ren) was often cited as reasons of rentership. One striking observation was that, opposed to conventional belief, house ownership was not the long-term goal of apartment owners and tenants due to the hassle-some obligations of maintaining a home in proper condition or supervising such maintenance, lack of need for large spaces (mostly due to limited number of family members), preference for availing convenient community services or obtaining greater social connections as apartment dwellers.

c) Marital Status and Household Structure: Most of the respondents that is sixty-five (out of seventy) are married, while four being widows (female) and one widower (male). Majority of the older apartment residents (fifty nine out of seventy) are from nuclear families presently living with only spouse in small size apartments, or sometimes with/ without spouse and child (ren)/ child (ren) in-law. Four out of seventy respondents live alone and the remaining seven respondents are from joint families (presently living with/without a spouse, children/ children-in-law and other relatives). Any household with more than five members is considered as joint family for the purpose of this study (Rajan & Kumar, 2003). When staying with married children, respondents stayed with married sons but none were staying with married daughters, but in some cases stayed close to married daughters for care or support. This is reflective of the popular notion in Asian societies that sons are the primary custodians of aged parents. Small sized apartments hardly instill any feeling of discomfort related to shortage of space among the elderly who, on the contrary, find large spaces "unnecessary" and "difficult to manage". The respondents expressed a clear preference for non-institutional living in familiar residential environment of home and neighborhood. In such a context, the size of the family becomes important in determining the social support received; the absence of support at home places greater responsibility on the quality on neighborhood support received. A mismatch between the support expected and the support received causes residential dissatisfaction among the apartment dwellers.

Residential Community and Built Environment as Determinants of Residential Satisfaction

a) Residential Community: Out of seventy respondents, sixty two of them reported that the most important characteristics of the residential community are support received from the community, cordial relationship with neighbors, presence of security and surveillance, absence of crime or noise or abandoned buildings or dark streets or rodents or garbage. The absence or presence of these had a direct bearing on their residential experience and satisfaction while the remaining eight respondents placed greater importance on home environment than neighborhood environment. Housing density was not reported as a problem by the elderly residents of apartments.

b) Built Environment: Talking about the relationship between residential satisfaction and the characteristics of the built environment fifty four out of seventy respondents reported that the building age, maintenance, cleanliness of the building premise, location of the building ensuring easy accessibility to services or shopping centers, presence of recreational facilities were important. Presence of private open spaces, closeness to the ground or lift facilities, subsidized building rent (for the tenants) and subsidized building maintenance charges (for the owners) were identified as other important factors for considering residential satisfaction.

Table 1. Denoting the Socio-demographic characteristics of the respondents (in percentage %) (N=70)

Age Group respondents		*No. of Gender*		*Marital Status*		*Educational Qualification*		*Monthly Household Income*		*Family Size*		
		M	*F*	*Married*	*Widow/ Widower*	*Upto HS*	*Graduate & above*	*MIG MIG*	*HIG HIG*	*Nuclea Nuclear*	*Joint Joint*	*Alone*
60+	82	39	43	78	04	03	79	36	07	72	04	06
70+	14	04	10	14	00	08	06	17	12	10	04	00
80+	4	03	01	01	03	00	04	06	05	02	02	00
Total	100	46	54	93	07	11	89	59	24	84	10	06

Note: M=Male, F= Female, HS=Higher Secondary, LIG=Low income groups, MIG= Middle income groups, HIG= High income groups. Source: Author's Primary Data

Residential Community and Built Environment as Determinants of Residential Satisfaction (Depicted in Order of Importance)	
Residentail Community	**Built Environment**
• Safety & Security	• Location
• Community Support	• Building Maintenance
• Cordial Neighbourhood Relations	• Difficult Stairs/Faulty Building Designs
• Absence of Garbage	• Cleanliness
• Presence of Street Lights/ Pavements	• Subsidized Rent/Maintenance Charges
• Absence of Rodents	• Building Age
• Absence of Noise	• Recreational Facilities
• Abandoned Buildings Around	• Floor Space (Apartment Size)

Fig 2: Showing determinants of residential satisfaction on the basis of characteristics of residential community and built environment ordered as most important to least important.

Source: Author's Primary Data

Findings of the present study contribute to the existing body of literature investigating the relationship between living environment and residential satisfaction among the urban elderly. Since the respondents have worked in the service sectors or are still engaged in occupation beyond retirement, most of them have earned enough to own the apartments they are currently residing in. Two patterns of household arrangements are predominant in the data collected: those living with only spouse and those living with spouse and children. However, since most of the respondents interviewed are currently residing with only spouse as their children are settled elsewhere, the study indicates that co-residence with children is gradually declining. Though this decline has somewhat placed greater importance on congenial neighborhood conditions for social support and overall satisfaction, not sharing space with children is not always indicative of intergenerational conflict or erosion of social values of caring for parents. The breakdown of joint family does not automatically make the elderly helpless, if they have enough financial assets. Living away from children may sometimes be a matter of situation, choice, and privacy needed by both the generations. More elderly men were reported to be living alone, either because they were economically better positioned or because they had better health condition compared to their female counterparts. Due to these factors, the respondents chosen for the study have indicated greater preference for living in easy to maintain small sized apartments as against large spaces in households which require "sufficient effort" to be invested for proper maintenance. As mentioned earlier, unlike younger people, the residential satisfaction of the apartment dwellers were not reported to be dependent on housing density or age segregated housing communities. This is mainly because living in spatially distant residences meant less scope to form social connections, especially in case of those suffering from physical decline or immobility. Those rarely meeting their neighbors thus reported greater loneliness and social isolation. Likewise, living in apartments with heterogeneous population was reported preferable as it increased the scope of interaction and support from diverse age groups. Apart from community support, the respondents also placed great importance on leading a life of safety without the fear of crime in neighborhood because many are of the opinion that old age makes a person more vulnerable to crimes. Noise was not a major problem for many as many usually lived in peaceful neighborhood while some reported hearing impairment. Since majority of the respondents belonged to the young elderly group of 60-65 years, they were in an overall good health condition and lived independently; while only a minority of them suffering from chronic health diseases. A large majority of the population being engaged in work, location of the building was reported as the most important characteristic of built environment. Absence of availability of transport and difficult accessibility to work places, markets or other community services, led to feelings of dissatisfaction and social exclusion. People have differential preferences and criteria to evaluate residential satisfaction. Despite the variously stated problems, and occasional incongruence between preferences and lived experience in residential environment, it was interesting to note that residents frequently expressed overall satisfaction with their residence at apartments that offered them with various amenities and community services.

Conclusion

Rapid urbanization not only introduce problem of improvised city spaces, but also add to the woes of the elderly population, a vast section of whom inadequate and uncertain livelihood. Migration not only creates problem of over-crowding in city spaces but is also indicative of decline in social support older people receive from their family. Older people have equal rights to a share to urban spaces and the right to be housed in congenial residential environment much like the younger population. In India, there are various laws to protect and advance the rights of the elderly but unfortunately not all are implemented in a way that would help enhance quality of life of the elderly. The limited coverage of old age schemes has only worsened with the accelerated growth in the number older adults in the country. Pondering over the best possible ways to allocate urban resources ensuring cost effective social security for the aged in India, might be quite challenging. Since older people's immediate home environment is as important as neighborhood environment, policy designing should pay careful attention to both indoor and outdoor living condition to minimize challenges and potential hazards to older persons' activities of daily living. Only ensuring them with equal access to civic spaces, resources and urban facilities might not be enough. Creating greater employment opportunities for the healthy aged, involving them in decision-making processes in formulating elderly friendly policies and encouraging them to play a part in the change might prove to be helpful.

References

Achenbaum, W. A. (2005). Ageing and Changing: International Historical Perspectives on Ageing. The Cambridge Handbook of Age and Ageing (Eds. M. L. Johnson, P. G. Coleman, T. B. L. Kirkwood, & V. L. Bengtson), pp. 21-29. Cambridge University Press.

Bowering, T. (2019). Ageing, Mobility and the City: Objects, Infrastructures and Practices in Everyday Assemblages of Civic Spaces in East London. Journal of Population Ageing https://doi.org/10.1007/s12062-019-9240-3

Buffel, T., Phillipson, C., & Boilard, S. R. (2019) Age-Friendly Cities and Communities: New Directions for Research and Policy. Encyclopedia of Gerontology and Population Aging (Eds. D. Gu, M. E. Dupre), pp. 1-10. Springer Nature Switzerland AG 2019. https://doi.org/10.1007/978-3-319-69892-2_1094-1

Buffel, T., Skyrme, J., & Phillipson, C. (2017). Connecting Research with Social Responsibility: Developing 'Age-Friendly' Communities in Manchester, UK. University Social Responsibility and Quality of Life A Global Survey of Concepts and Experiences (Eds. D. T.L. Shek, & R. M. Hollister), pp. 99-120. Springer

Byrnes, M., Lichtenberg, P. A., & Lysack, C. (2006). Environmental Press, Aging in Place, and Residential Satisfaction of Urban Older Adults. Sociological Practice Special Joint Issue with "Journal of Applied Sociology", 8 (2), 50-76.

Dahlberg, L. (2019). Ageing in a changing place: a qualitative study of neighbourhood exclusion. Ageing & Society, 1-19. doi:10.1017/S0144686X1900045X

Dapaah, K. A., & Wong, G. K. M. (2001). Housing and the elderly in Singapore - financial and quality of life implications of ageing in place. Journal of Housing and the Built Environment, 16 (2), 153-178.

Dey, A. B. (2010). Ageing and Well-being. Ageing and Health in India (Eds. C. S. Johnson, & S. I. Rajan), pp. 21-35. Rawat Publications

Dixit, U., & Goyal, V. C. (2015). Technology Support in Active Ageing. Caring for the Elderly: Social Gerontology in the Indian Context (Eds. T. Paltasingh and R. Tyagi), pp. 245-263. Sage Publications India Private Limited.

Erickson, J., & Johnson, M. (2011). Internet Use and Psychological Wellness during Late Adulthood. Canadian Journal on Ageing, 30(2), 197-209.

Foley, D. L. (1980). The Sociology of Housing. Annual Review of Sociology, 6, 457-478

Grum, (2019). Differences in perceptions of the living environment by respondent age. Urbani izziv, 30 (2), 85-94. doi: 10.5379/urbani-izziv-en-2019-30-02-002

Heide, L. A.., Loek, A., Willems, C. G., Speeuwenberg, M. D., Rietman, J., & de Witte, L. P. (2012). Implementation of CareTV in care for the elderly: the effects of feelings of loneliness and safety and future challenges. Technology and Disability, 24(4), 283-291.

James III, R. N. (2008). Residential Satisfaction of Elderly Tenants in Apartment Housing. Social Indicators Research, 89 (3), 421-437.

Khan, A. (2015). Bridging Inter-generational Gap through School Education. Caring for the Elderly: Social Gerontology in the Indian Context (Eds. T. Paltasingh and R. Tyagi), pp. 225-244. Sage Publications India Private Limited.

Kaulagekar, A. (2007). Ageing and Social Support: A Study of Low-income Urban Elderly in Pune. Indian Anthropologist, 37 (2), 45-53

Kraus, H. (1952). Housing Our Older Citizens. The Annals of the American Academy of Political and Social Science, Social Contribution by the Aging, 279, 126-138

Kumar, P., & Khan, A. M. (2015). Prospective Approach to Healthy Ageing. Caring for the Elderly: Social Gerontology in the Indian Context (Eds. T. Paltasingh and R. Tyagi), pp. 157-172. Sage Publications India Private Limited.

Manfredini, M., & Breschi, M. (2013). Living Arrangements and the Elderly: An Analysis of Old-Age Mortality by Household Structure in Casalguidi, 1819-1859. Demography, 50 (5), 1593-1613.

Oswald, F., Hieber, A., Wahl, H.-W., & Mollenkopf, H. (2005). Ageing and person-environment fit in different urban neighbourhoods. European Journal of Ageing, 2 (2), 88-97.

doi: 10.1007/s10433-005-0026-5

Peek, S. T. M., Aarts, S., & Wouters, E. J. M. (2015). Can Smart Home Technology Deliver on the Promise of Independent Living? A Critical Reflection Based on the Perceptions of Older Adults. Handbook of Smart Homes, Health Care and Well- Being. Springer International Publishing Switzerland. doi: 10.1007/978-3-319-01904-8_41-1

Perez, F. R., Mayoralas, G. F., Rivera, F. E. P., & Abuin, J. M. R. (2001). Ageing in Place: Predictors of the Residential Satisfaction of Elderly. Social Indicators Research, 54 (2), 173-208

Phillips, D. R., Siu, O. L., Yeh, A. G. O., & Cheng, K. H. C. (2004). Factors influencing older persons' residential satisfaction in big and densely populated cities in Asia: a Case Study in Hong Kong. Ageing International, 29 (1), 46-70.

Rajan, S. I., & Kumar, S. (2003). Living Arrangements among Indian Elderly: New Evidence from National Family Health Survey. Economic and Political Weekly, 38 (1), 75-80.

Tyagi, R., & Paltasingh, T. (2015). Ageing Well and Way Forward. Caring for the Elderly: Social Gerontology in the Indian Context (Eds. T. Paltasingh and R. Tyagi), pp. 264-280. Sage Publications India Private Limited.

Chapter 7

An Analogical Study Between Modern City Spaces and Huxleys's Brave New World

Swastideepa Mazumder

Introduction

Cities, the centers of knowledge, innovation and specialization of production and services. facilitate creative thinking and innovation. High concentration of people in cities generates more opportunities for interaction and communication, promotes creative thinking, creates knowledge spillovers and develops new ideas and technologies. Cities provide more opportunities for learning and sharing. They facilitate trade and commerce by providing super market areas. Cities serve as production and services centers because the production of many goods and services is more efficient in a high-density urban environment. They provide consumers with more choices of goods and services. Cities are the agents of social, cultural, economic, technologic and political changes and advancement. Cities play a pivotal role in economic development providing economies of scale, agglomeration, and localization; besides efficient infrastructure and services through density and concentration in transportation, communications, power, human interactions, water and sanitation services. They attract talents and skilled labor that allow specialization in knowledge, skills, and management capabilities possible.

To the most unfortunate turn of events over years, these cities are expected to result in major unmatched growth of human population giving rise to economic and social stratification , environmental degradation and scarcity of major natural resources, transportation clogging etc. The world's urban population grew from 220 million to 2.8 billion in the 20th century. The next few decades will see an unprecedented scale of urban growth. By 2030, this is expected to expand to about 5 billion. Such rapid urban expansion will be particularly notable in Africa and Asia where the urban population will double between 2000 and 2030. By 2030, the towns and cities of the developing world will make up 81 per cent of urban humanity.

In the light of this, I would like to bring concept of the urban society as foreseen by Aldous Huxley in his novel, *Brave New World* (1932). In the novel we learn about the city of '*World State*' in a futuristic London in the year AF (After Ford) 632 where citizens engineered through artificial wombs and mostly technological interventions are soon conditioned through various indoctrination programmes into pre-determined classes based on their intelligence. The residents of the '*World State*' consume their almost universal drug '*soma*' to create a state of delusion which clouds them from the reality of present replacing them with jovial hallucinations, directing to promote social stability. Amidst this dystopian society, we find John, a sexually reproduced human, and an alien to the '*Brave New World*', who finds solace in reading Shakespeare. However he is the moral exception to the dystopian society's aimless functioning who ultimately becomes a martyr, further setting him apart from the apathetic world by his intense passions and humanity.

Persuaded by the fact that stability was the "primal and ultimate need" Huxley went on to show the widely felt anxieties, particularly the fear of losing individuality in the fast paced world of the future .In this paper I would like to discuss the role, city plays in the growth of a nation thereby catering economic stability; how these city spaces are going to face the upcoming challenges and would strive for survival among the odds whereby we can expect Huxley's forestalled future not to be a probable scene in the coming decades.

Role of the cities in shaping the Global Economy

Cities are the hubs for economic expansion. Following is some of the basic points designed for the better understanding of their roles:

- Cities or urban spaces determine the transportation and communication technologies in terms of both cost and quality. Cities become larger and more vital as the transport and communication technologies develop further. On one hand transport and communication technologies enable many forms of economic and social interaction to occur over greater distances and spaces; on the other hand, they enhance the need for proximity. Different economic activities are interconnected through their transactional or network relationships to each other and to the rest of the world.

- Cities provide a better environment for the growth of semi-skilled and skilled labors. Large city spaces often offer complex skills of labor, technology, services, training and information. Cities are instrumental in providing conditions for acquiring economically useful knowledge in a timely fashion through human relationships and interactions and being able to unravel it in meaningful ways. Both efficiency and creativity are faster to acquire in urban spaces, as the cost of transaction decreases as distance decreases.

- Vast areas of modern economy involve activities where enormous uncertainty prevails and ensure mutual interactions, which is particularly true to high order economic activities. For instance, the highly technological industries and financial services where we encounter changing –product oriented or client-oriented goods and services requiring firms to be organized so as to change the mix of skills and resources that they bring to each particular tasks at various levels of productivity.

- The vital role of a city lies in building the nation's economy. In a way we come to a clearer conclusion by observing the Gross Domestic Product incurred by a city. This particular role of the city is more significant in the developing countries than the developed countries. For instance, as we shall from the following figure, that Sao Paulo has 10.5 percent of population and generates 19.5 percent of GDP. Shanghai, with a 1.2 percent of population generates 2.9 percent of GDP. Buenos Aires, with a 32.5 percent of population produces 63.2 percent of GDP. Mumbai, with 2 percent of population, accounts for 6.3 percent of GDP. Nairobi, with 9 percent of population, generates 20 percent of GDP, Dar es Salaam, with 7.9 percent of population, accounts for 14.9 percent of GDP. In Shanghai, Manila, Brasilia, Cape Town, Karachi and Nairobi, cities generate more than 100 percent higher GDP than their population share. In Dhaka, Yangon, Chittagong, Khartoum, Mumbai, cities generate more than 200 percent higher GDP than their population share. In Addis Ababa, it generates more than 360 percent higher GDP than its population share. In Hanoi, it produces more than 460 percent higher GDP than its population share. In Kinshasha and Kabul, cities generate more than 500 percent higher GDP than their population share. Estimates of the contribution of cities to total GDP in India range from 60 percent to 80 percent.

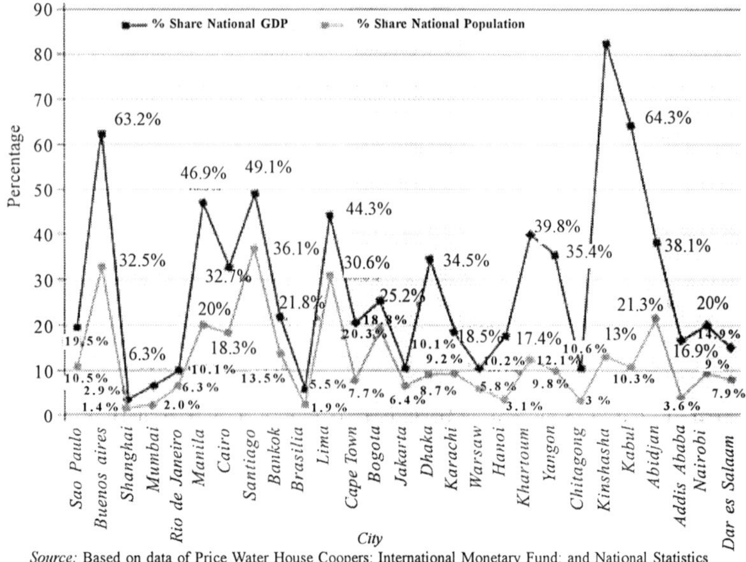

Source: Based on data of Price Water House Coopers: International Monetary Fund: and National Statistics

Figure 1: Share of National Population and GDP in Key Cities in Developing Countries in 2008

- Various medical and health facilities and educational institutions, providing greater scopes of courses and trainings in a wide range of subjects and skills, are found in abundance in the city spaces. This results in *migration* from rural or sub-urban areas. Also, which further results in *urbanization*.

Urbanization

Before we indulge into the topic of Urbanization, its causes and effects, let us first know what these terms exactly mean:

> *Migration* - Migration is the movement of people from one place to another with the intentions of settling, permanently or temporarily, at a new location. Migration is influenced by economic growth and development and by technological change (Marshall et al., 2009) and possibly also by conflict and social disruption. It is driven by pull factors that attract people to urban areas and push factors that drive people away from the countryside.
>
> *Urbanization* - Urbanization refers to the population shift from rural to urban areas, the decrease in the proportion of people living in rural areas, and the ways in which societies adapt to this change. It is predominantly the process by which towns and cities are formed and become larger as more people begin living and working in central areas.

Migration is also caused for a various other factor such as better employment opportunities. As maximum number of industries are located in the city belts paying comparatively high amounts of wages than the lesser paid or unpaid jobs of the villages.

People are moving away from rural areas also because of environmental changes, droughts, floods, lack of availability of sufficiently productive land, and other pressures on rural livelihoods.

All we can say is that migration is one of the most important causes of urbanization. In 1960, the global urban population was 34% of the total; however, by 2014 the urban population accounted for 54% of the total and continues to grow. By 2050 the proportion living in urban areas is expected to reach 66% (UNDESA, 2014). (Figure 2)

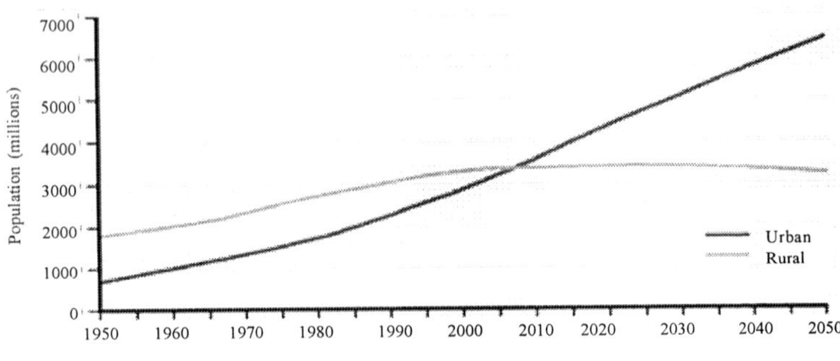

Source:(UNDESA, 2014)

Impacts of Urbanization

Rapid surge in population and unplanned growth create an urban sprawl with negative economic, social, physical and mental and environmental consequences.

Economic consequences

a. Economic effects include a dramatic hike and change in costs, often pricing the local working class out of the market, including such functionaries as employees of the local municipalities. For example, Eric Hobsawm's book *The Age of Revolution: 1789–1848* (published 1962 and 2005) chapter 11, stated "Urban development in our period [1789–1848] was a gigantic process of class segregation, which pushed the new laboring poor into great morasses of misery outside the centers of government, business, and the newly specialized residential areas of the bourgeoisie. The almost universal European division into a 'good' west end and a 'poor' east end of large cities developed in this period."

b. The developing countries are being affected by similar problems nowadays, with rising inequality resulting from rapid urbanization trends. Speaking of this we may refer the unequal conditions seen in India, with one–eighth of the urban population living in slums which counts to approximately 9 million households, and is expected to increase by 2millions annually (National Sample Survey Organization, 2013). One reason behind this impact is vast migration from rural areas of

India towards the more urban cities. In figure 3, we see an aerial view of Mumbai's Dharavi slum, which is a result of lack of jobs with insufficient household spaces. The last decade has seen little growth in jobs, exaggerating the problem to an ever greater extent, decline in the manufacturing sector and poor quality and access to education has caused much lower opportunities for employment. Speaking internationally, in Addis Ababa, a report in 2008 found that 80% of the houses in the city were classed as slums due to the physical deterioration of its housing, overcrowding, high density, poor access and lack of infrastructure services. (Figure 4)

Figure 3. **Dharavi slum in Mumbai, India.**

Figure 4. Urban slum in Addis Ababa, the capital of Ethiopia

c. Urbanization and poverty are intertwined with each other. According to the global monetary report countries that have 40% or less people living in cities have significantly lower income level and higher poverty rates. Urbanization reduces poverty since it generates new opportunities. For example, China has chalked out plans to make urbanization, the engine for future growth (Spence et al. 2008). Economists in China found that people who live in the cities earn more money than the people who live in the country sides. Thus. it can be comprehended that urbanization is linked with national income as seen in most developed countries which are highly urbanized.

- Social consequences- The overcrowding of the city spaces by urbanization places stresses on existing social norms and services. Crime, prostitution, drug abuse and street children are all negative effects of urbanization. The simplest explanation is that areas with a higher population density are surrounded by greater availability of goods which makes committing crimes in those areas more feasible. Some wealthy cities also encounter a rise in property crime and a decrease in violent crime. Also there tends to be a lack of social support for children in school and home by their hard-working, mostly poor, parents. Inadequate income, overcrowded housing and poor living conditions create a yielding ground for the development of violence. Violence is more visible in the cities than in rural areas and it affects people's everyday life, their movements and the use of public transport. Crime in the city can create a sense of insecurity within its dwellers. This unsafe feeling in city streets separates residential areas into higher-income and lower-income groups, which reduces the sense of community and forms areas with dissimilar incomes, costs and security levels. Factors responsible for an increase in the number of crimes in cities include per capita income, income inequality, and overall population size. There is also a little association between unemployment rate, police expenditures and crime. The presence of crime also has the ability to multiply more crimes. These areas have less social cohesion and therefore less social control. This is evident in the geographical regions that crime occurs in. As most crime tends to cluster in city centers, the further the distance from the center of the city, the lower the occurrence of crimes are.

Environmental consequences-

a. The presence of urban heat islands is a major environmental effect of urbanization along with the process of eutrophication in water bodies. When heavy shower occurs in these large cities, the rain filters down the pollutants such as CO_2 and other greenhouse gases in the air onto the ground below. Then, those chemicals are washed directly into rivers, streams, and oceans, causing a decline in water quality and damaging marine ecosystems.

Urban Heat Island- An urban heat island is formed when industrial and cityspaces produce and retain heat. Much of the solar energy that reaches rural areas is consumed by evaporation of water from vegetation and soil. In cities, where there are less vegetation and exposed soil, most of the sun's energy is instead absorbed by buildings and asphalt; leading to higher surface temperatures. Vehicles, factories, and industrial and domestic heating and cooling units release even more heat. As a result, cities are often 1 to 3 °C (1.8 to 5.4 °F) warmer than surrounding landscapes.

Eutrophication- Eutrophication is a process which causes hypoxic water conditions and algal blooms that may be harmful to the survival of aquatic life. Detrimental algal blooms, which produce dangerous toxins, thrive in eutrophic environments that are also rich in nitrogen and phosphorus. In these ideal conditions, they overtake surface water, making it difficult for other organisms to receive sunlight and nutrients. Overgrowth of algal blooms causes a decrease in overall water quality and disrupts the natural balance of aquatic ecosystems. Furthermore, as algal blooms die, CO_2 is produced, causing a more acidic environment, a process known as acidification.

b. Urban Food Waste is one of the other major challenges of over population in cities. The increase of food waste can raise environmental concerns such as increase production of methane gases and attraction of disease vectors. Landfills are the third leading cause of the release of methane, causing a concern on its impact to our ozone and on the health of individuals. Amassing of food waste causes increased fermentation, which increases the risk of rodent and bug migration. An increase in migration of disease vectors creates greater potential of disease spreading to humans.

c. There is a strong interlink between increasing urbanization and declining biodiversity (Paucharda et al. 2006). The increasing population is a catalyst for the expansion of urban areas, which in turn increases the demand for natural resources, for example fossil fuels and timber. This inevitably results in the destruction of habitats. In the United Kingdom there is an increasing human population density, and it was found that within the surrounding urbanized areas, 35% of scarce plant species had become extinct as a direct result in the increase of urban development (Czech et al. 2000).

Psychological consequences

a. Urbanization affects mental health through the influence of increased stressors and factors such as overcrowded and polluted environment, high levels of violence, and reduced social support. Impact of urbanization is associated with an increase in mental disorders. The reason being that movement of people to urban area needs more facilities to be made available and infrastructure to grow. This does not happen in alignment with the increase of population. As a result, lack of adequate infrastructure increases the risk of poverty and exposure to environmental adversities. Further this also decreases social support (Desjarlais *et al.*, 1995) as the nuclear families increase in number. Poor families experience environmental and psychological adversity which increases their vulnerability to mental disorders (Patel, 2001).

b. A report by World Health Organization (WHO) has specified that mental disorders account for nearly 12% of the global burden of disease. By 2020, these will account for nearly 15% of disability-adjusted life-years (DALYs) lost to illness.

Incidentally, the burden of mental disorders is maximal in young adults, which is considered to be the most productive age of the population. Developing countries are likely to see a disproportionately large increase in the burden attributable to mental disorders in the coming decades (WHO Mental Health Context 2003).

c. The range of disorders and deviancies associated with urbanization is at large: depression, dementia, substance abuse, alcoholism, crime, family disintegration, and alienation are some of those. Speaking of psychiatric disorders, anxiety and depression are more prevalent among urban women than men and, are believed to be more prevalent in poor than in non-poor urban neighborhoods (Naomar Almeida-Filho *et al* 2004).

d. There is a need to create awareness about mental illness across all sections of the society. Urbanization is thus seen as a natural corollary of growth. Awareness about its impact on health and more so on mental health will act as a facilitator of change in growing economies.

Urbanization has its parts of pros and cons, but this ever-increasing population of the cities has left us with a big question mark regarding the future of these city spaces. It seems with the constant struggle to form an utopian society, we are miserably failing to form a dystopian society. In order to make this situation procurable to a larger scope of readers, I would like to bring a literary perspective to this highly serious economic and environmental issue.

Aldous Huxley's Brave New World was inspired by H.G. Wells's utopian novels, including A *Modern Utopia* (1905), and *Men Like Gods* (1923). Wells's hopeful vision of the future's possibilities gave Huxley the idea to begin writing a parody of the novels, which became *Brave New World*. Unlike the most popular optimistic utopian novels of the time, Huxley sought to provide a frightening vision of the future. Huxley referred to *Brave New World* as a "negative utopia", somewhat influenced by Wells's own *The Sleeper Awakes* (dealing with subjects like corporate tyranny and behavioral conditioning) and the works of D.H. Lawrence. The events of the Depression of

U.K in 1931, with its mass unemployment and the abandonment of the gold currency standard, persuaded Huxley to assert that stability was the "primal and ultimate need" if civilization was to survive the present crisis Huxley used the setting and characters in this science fiction novel to express widely felt anxieties, particularly the fear of losing individual identity in the fast-paced world of the future.

Aldous Huxley's Brave New World is set in 2540 AD in Georgian Calendar, which the novel identifies as the year AF 632. AF stands for "After Ford," as Henry Ford's assembly line is revered as god-like; this era began when Ford introduced his Model-T . This novel efficiently examines a futuristic society, called the '*World State*', that revolves around science and productivity. In this society, emotions and individuality are conditioned out of children at a primal age, and there are no lasting relationships because "every one belongs to everyone else" (a common '*World State'* dictum), a hypnopaedic suggestion discouraging exclusivity in relationships with friends and families. So to speak in this society, everyone is everyone else as well. All the fetal conditionings, hypnopaedic in nature along with the power of convention molds each individual of the society into an interchangeable part worthy enough only for the purpose of running the society smoothly. Even love, acknowledging and cherishing another's unique identity represents a threat to stability founded on uniformity. The dystopia's alternative, recreational sex is deliberately designed to blur the distinctions among lovers and between emotions and urges, finding its social and ritual expression called "Orgy-Porgy." In such a world uniqueness is uselessness and uniformity is bliss, for social stability is the goal.

In his 1946 Foreword to *Brave New World*, Huxley stated that the "theme of *Brave New World* is not the advancement of science as such; it is the advancement of science as it affects human individuals". *Brave New World* evokes the themes to portray the use of technology to control society, the incompatibility of happiness and truth, the perils of an over powerful state, individuality, happiness and its agencies. I shall discuss how Huxley has accentuated the future society and its norms which are very much dissimilar to the present ones.

As mentioned earlier this futuristic urban society has turned mechanical, devoid of feelings with the flourishing technology. We come to know from the progressing novel about the biochemical technology that makes the production of virtually identical human beings, possible, and in doing so we are introduced to Huxley's theme of individuality under assault. The normal human development is arrested by Bokanovsky's process, promoting a dozen identical eggs deliberately deprived of their unique, individual natures and so making overt processes for controlling them unnecessary. In the *Brave New World* society, embryos are classified into five groups before they are born forming a caste system of the superiors – Alphas and Betas; and inferiors- Gammas, Deltas and Epsilons. To create the top group biologically superior sperms are chose to fertilize biologically superior ova, which then receive excellent prenatal treatment. While on the other hand the lower castes which include the majority of the unborn children come from inferior sperms and eggs.

The Controllers of the World State strives to make citizens love servitude in various methods. One of them is clearly the individual formations by various scientific processes, secondly hypnopaedia. Hypnopaedic slogans and solidarity services encourage the dwellers to think of themselves as the part of the whole, and are sent to the islands when they get "too self-consciously individual to fit into community life". Clearly the society has learned to teach morals and values to its members in order to promote 'community, identity and stability'.

The third way to establish stability in the society is to use the chemical persuasion by encouraging the people to use '*soma*'. In Huxley's dystopia, the drug '*soma'* also serves to keep individuals from experiencing the stressful negative effects of conflicts that the society cannot prevent. Pain and stress, grief and humiliation, disappointment representing uniquely individual reactions to conflict still occur sometimes in the brave new world. The people of the 'brave new world' solve their conflict problems by swallowing a few tablets or taking an extended *soma*-holiday, which removes or sufficiently masks the negative feelings and emotions that other, more creative, problem-solving techniques might have and which cuts off the possibility of action that might have socially disruptive or revolutionary results. The society, therefore, encourages everyone to take '*soma*' as a means of social control by eliminating the effects of conflict and achieving social stability.

The Controllers promote self-indulgence as a fourth way. They provide the citizens with an assortment of games, movies called '*feelies*', the cabaret and solidarity services. Sexual freedom is people's biggest form of self-indulgence, which is made acceptable by the abolition of families. Scientific advancements are used to make sexual promiscuities by sterilizing most women. In spite of the fact that the leaders promote sexual activities, they do not want the masses to experience any strong passionate feeling/love that causes instability.

In order to have stability which is the basis for happiness in utopia, the Controller claims that art, religion, scientific progress and ultimately freedom must all be sacrificed.

To this way of living, a character stands out as an exception, who was born naturally of a mother, with no infant conditioning, and therefore also unknown to the norms of World State. He is John, the Savage. He represents a unique human being in the novel with an identity and relationship unlike any other character in the novel. He is rejected and disconnected by the Savage Reservation of the Malpais or of London where he grew up. His only society is Shakespeare's imaginative world, a realm he inhabits with passion and misguided idealism. John's extensive knowledge of Shakespeare's works serves him in several important ways for it enables him to verbalize his own complex emotions and reactions, it provides him with a framework from which to criticize World State values, and it provides him with language that allows him to hold his own against the formidable rhetorical skill of Mustapha Mond (the most powerful and intelligent proponent of the World State) during their confrontation. On the other hand, John's insistence on viewing the world through Shakespearean eyes sometimes blinds him to the reality of other characters, notably Lenina (a technician, in love with John, part of the 30% of the female population that are not freemartins or sterile women), who, in his mind, is alternately a heroine and a "strumpet," neither of which label is quite appropriate to her. John is intensely moral according to a code that he has been taught by Shakespeare and life in Malpais but is also naïve; his views are as imported into his own consciousness as are the hypnopaedic messages of World State citizens. John's rejection of the shallow happiness of the World State, his inability to reconcile his love and lust for Lenina, and even his eventual suicide all reflect themes from Shakespeare. Shakespeare embodies all of the human and humanitarian values that have been abandoned in the World State and John himself is a Shakespearean character in such a world.

John asserts that the technological wonders and consumerism of the World State are poor substitutes for individual freedom, human dignity and personal integrity. He is revolted by the poverty of art and culture in the 'brave new world' society. The phrase "brave new world" takes on an increasingly bitter, ironic, and pessimistic tone as he becomes more knowledgeable about the State. After his mother's death, he becomes deeply distressed with grief, surprising onlookers in the hospital. He then shuns himself from society and attempts to purify himself of "sin" (desire), but is finally unable to do so. John's participation in the final orgy and his suicide at the end of the novel can be seen as the result of his own imperfect understanding as well as the inhuman forces of the brave new world, of an insanity created by the fundamental conflict between his values and the reality of the world around him.

In presenting a world where society has been perfected and people live happily and peacefully, *Brave New World* is an example of a utopian novel. Aldous Huxley literalizes this concept in the '*World State*' of *Brave New World*, imagining a future where genetic engineering and psychological conditioning have created a society of contented and happy citizens. Because each person in '*World State*' has been programmed to be perfectly suited to his or her occupation and to pity members of different social orders, drives like ambition, dissatisfaction, and envy no longer exist. Frequent, indiscriminate sexual activity prevents strong emotions of love and jealousy, and any momentary feelings other than contentment are relieved with drugs. In some ways '*World State*' does appear preferable to our society, as disease, aging, crime, depression, and wars are all things of the past. Unlike the real world, less advantaged characters in World State have no sense of injustice about their lives in relation to their more privileged counterparts, and the society exists in harmony.

While suggesting many societal ills may be solved through developments in science and psychology, Huxley also implicitly satirizes the idea of utopias. The citizens of the '*World State*' are happy, but they also lead meaningless lives, and most of the main characters have the sneaking suspicion that their way of life is not as idyllic as they've been taught. The absence of all art, history, religion, and familial ties suggests that their lives, while painless, are also empty. The necessity of the drug '*soma*' to keep citizens compliant and submissive indicates their utopia is an artificial state that needs constant maintenance, and left to their own devices humans would soon revert to fighting, crime, war, and misery. The tightly bound caste system, in which the majority of society is genetically engineered to serve a tiny, privileged minority, is morally reprehensible, even if the lower classes have been conditioned to accept and even embrace their oppression. Though universal happiness seems utopian, Huxley exposes the disturbing steps necessary to achieve it, and suggests that pain, suffering, and despair are integral to personal autonomy.

In presenting a so-called utopia that leads the most intelligent and free-thinking character (John) to suicide, *Brave New World* can also be considered an example of dystopian fiction, although its vision of the future is less obviously bleak than many dystopian novels. Developed in direct critique of utopian novels, which posited those societal problems were solvable, dystopian novels maintain that human beings' inherent flaws doom them to misery. In *Brave New World,* the only truly content characters are those who have blinded themselves to the reality of their situation by taking drugs. As soon as characters stop using drugs, they find their lives depressingly devoid of meaning. John, the most enlightened character in the novel, is so horrified by the '*World State*' he ends up killing himself. Huxley's work is different from dystopian novels such as George Orwell's *1984,* which was directly influenced by Huxley's ideas and portrays a society plagued by violence, hunger, and mass surveillance. In many dystopian novels there is a sinister secret to the government's method of controlling its citizens. In *Brave New World,* there is no secret – the government openly controls the masses through the distribution of soma, which they willingly and eagerly consume. Though there is little violence in the book, its vision is as disturbing, bleak, and cautionary as other dystopian novels.

Modern city spaces getting over populated at an increasing rate is a big problem to address. But its growth trends made me feel that perhaps we are going to face a life and a society as portrayed in *Brave New World*. All we can wish is that urbanization to be beneficial to the country's economy as well as the society. The society is not expected to be poignantly scientific or technological. We do not want our standard of living to be just comfortable with more luxuries or pleasures at the cost of imagination, love and the warmth of our relationships. Our society in the face of scientific advancements and the development of infrastructures are not to be expected to give up arts, humanities or religion or stop being creative. The modern issues of committing crime upon women are unimaginable to reach to a point where women are treated as the second-class citizens as done in Huxley's dystopia. We do not want a society where men and women are the victims of an emotionless living. We do not wish for a life, where we have to take the support of *soma*-like drugs to cloud ourselves from the harsh realities of our lives. We would rather want a society of sustainable developments with achievable goals in our minds, with equal participation of all strata of our society and able to face our failures with a hope to further make it a success. Subsequently we can think of achieving proper growth of a nation in the face of overpopulation.

References

Higgins, Charles, Regina Higgins, and Warren Paul. *CliffsNotes on Brave New World.* 31 Jul 2020

"Impacts of Urbanization." *Economic Impacts-Impacts of Urbanization-Google Sites*, sites.google.com/site/impactsofurbanisation/economic-impacts.

Lohnes, K. "Brave New World Summary Context and Reception." *Encyclopaedia Britannica*, www.britannica.com/topic/Brave-New-World.

Retrieved from </literature/b/brave-new-world/book-summary>.

SparkNotesEditor. "Brave New World Study Guide." *Brave New World-Study Guide*, 2005, Retrieved from www.sparknotes.com/lit/bravenew/.

Srivastava, Kalpana. (2009) "Urbanization and Mental Health ." *Urbanization and Mental Health-NCBI*, doi:10.4103/0972-6748.64028.

Urbanisation: Trends, Causes and Effects." *Study Session 5 Urbanisation: Trends, Causes and Effects*, www.open.edu/openlearncreate/mod/oucontent/view.php?id=79940&printable=1

Zhang, Xing Quan. (2011) "The Economic Role of Cities." *United Nations Human Settlements Programme*, UN-HABITAT., urban-intergroup.eu/wp-content/files_mf/economicroleofcities_unhabitat11.pdf